WHY NOT

Celebrate!

WHY NOT

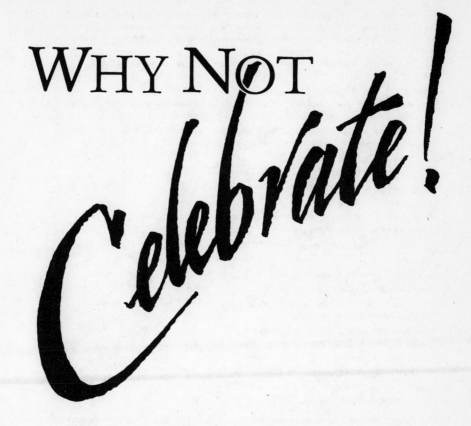

Celebrate!

Sara Wenger Shenk

a Budding Tree title

Good Books

Intercourse, PA 17534

Acknowledgments

The publishers have attempted to locate and contact the owners of all copyright material included. If any item has been used without proper credit or permission, whether through oversight, lack of current address or the use of material thought to be in the public domain, Good Books will gladly make necessary corrections in all subsequent editions.

The author and publishers wish to thank the following people and organizations for permission to use material:

Celebration for "'Sanna," © 1975.

The Central Conference of American Rabbis (Reform) for permission to include a prayer contributed by Rabbi Herbert Bronstein from the *Union Prayer Book* in "A Family Peace Prayer Service."

Geoffrey Chapman, a division of Cassell Ltd., 35 Red Lion Square, London, WC1R 4SG, England, for "St. Patrick's Breastplate (Bunessan)" from *New Hymns for All Seasons* By Fr. JamesQuinn, S. J., © 1969.

Linas Brown for "The Blessing of Houses."

Larry Clark for "Birthday Celebration" and "Birthday Liturgy."

The Episcopal Peace Fellowship for "A Litany of Intercession for Peace."

Anne Gavit for "The Moving Song."

Harper & Row Publishers, Inc., for permission to quote from *The Long Loneliness* by Dorothy Day, © 1952.

Allan Howe for "A Family Peace Prayer Service" and "Liturgy to Remember."

Jan-Lee Music for "Let There Be Peace on Earth," © 1955, 1983.

Mike and Marianne Lembeck for permission to quote their comments in "Baby Dedication."

Marcia Lind and Reba Place Church for "Hosanna, Son of David," © 1975.

Nancy Miner Martin and Reba Place Church for "Father, Bless This House," © 1978.

Paulist Press for "Light" from *Bread Blessed and Broken* ed. John Mossi, © 1974, and permission to quote from *Community and Growth* by Jean Vanier, © 1979.

Reba Place Church for "St. Patrick: Missionary to the Irish."

James A. Stringham, M.D., for "How the Lord Told Me to Deal with the Grief after My Wife's Sudden Death after 56 years of Marriage," © 1986. Used by permission.

The United Synagogue Commission on Jewish Education for "Peace Be Unto You," © 1950.

Conrad Wetzel and Reba Place Church for "Our Hearts We Lift."

World's Student Christian Federation for "Each Morning Brings," text © 1951.

Except for certain quotations from the King James Version within contributed exercises, scripture quotations in this publication are from the Holy Bible, New International Version. Copyright © 1973, 1978, 1984, International Bible Society. Psalm 103:1-22 in the "Service of Confession and Forgiveness" is quoted, with permission, from the Revised Standard Version.

Library of Congress Cataloging-in-Publication Data
Shenk, Sara Wenger, 1953-
   Why not celebrate!

   Bibliography: p.
   1. Fasts and feasts. 2. Rites and ceremonies.
3. Reba Place Fellowship (Evanston, Ill.) I. Title.
BV43.S53 1987   249   87-80804
ISBN 0-934672-45-8 (pbk.)

WHY NOT CELEBRATE!

Design by Craig N. Heisey
Published by Good Books, Intercourse, PA 17534

Table of Contents

Preface

Dear Friends,

The spring rains began in earnest today, washing the last dirty snow from the streets and gutters. With some effort and more imagination I spied a hint of green grass beneath the frost-scorched mat of brown. A balmy breeze brought whiffs of damp earth through the window, evoking a memory of spring. I longed to respond with hallelujahs and hugs all around. It was only last week that on awakening, four-year-old Timothy's first mournful words each morning were "Oh, I can't wait 'til spring." And his mother was too much in tune with his sentiments for everyone's good. Winter's inner city grimness weighed down heavily this year.

Oh, I know winter isn't through with us yet. It's only early March in northern Illinois. But the promise of reprieve blew in through my open window today and I felt like celebrating. I baked a cherry pie— my hurrah to the rhythmic reassurance of the returning seasons. At the dinner table our family of four enjoyed last year's sour cherries, slightly embellished, while hailing this year's hint of more to come.

I like to celebrate! At the same time, I'm not much for elaborate productions. I'm not the type to go in for decorating the whole house for an occasion. The mere thought of preparing a Thanksgiving or Christmas dinner makes my blood pressure hit the ceiling. I resist, with a passion, doing things out of obligation or to elicit marveling accolades from my guests. Simplicity is the saving grace that enables me to celebrate meaningfully without madness.

I know there are folks who have a flair for festivity, folks who can pull off an enormous bash and love every minute of the preparations. Not me! My style is to search for sacred meaning within the small, everyday moments, to revere the silences, the clasped hands, the broken loaf, the first evening star. One can compose a symphony of simple beauty out of the stuff that fills an ordinary day. By God's grace, that which is common becomes sacred and points to the reality of God in our midst.

Most of us walk about with well-muffled senses, senses that for want of exercise have grown sluggish and dull. Even those of us who think we have keen vision see only "through a glass darkly." But when the gift of sight *is* given, we ache to respond. When taste, touch, sound, smell and story awake our sleepy stupor, we long to celebrate. But how? Who can teach us? What traditions can guide us?

My husband and I have two sons. Joseph and Timothy are growing up in a very different world from that in which Gerald and I spent our childhood. Theirs is a city-apartment environment, peopled with folks from every conceivable ethnic and religious (or nonreligious) background. Their friends at school talk of dinosaurs, robots, the Chicago Bears and computer software programs.

Our world was peopled fairly consistently with ethnically homogeneous Mennonites. Both of our family lines can be traced in an unbroken chain back to Swiss-German Anabaptist folk who fled persecution in Europe to settle in William Penn's peaceful woods. Our childhood friends talked about John Deere tractors, ice-skating parties, small-game hunting and summer Bible school.

Mennonites who hail from the left wing of the 16th century Reformation have traditionally stood somewhat apart from mainstream Protestantism and Catholicism. The desire to be nonconformed to the world has shaped Mennonite lifestyle and theology, giving them a distinctly separatist flavor. As more and more of us have moved from our rural enclaves to the cities, however, we are searching for new ways to be "in the world but not of it."

Gerald and I still consider ourselves Mennonites. In fact, our loyalty to the faith of our mothers and fathers runs very deep. But when confronted by a barrage of other traditions and voices in our urban environs, we are forced as never before to decide, consciously and deliberately, how to pass on the faith to the next generation. How do we celebrate peoplehood? How do we celebrate God's good earth? How do our children develop a sense of identity that runs deeper than the latest fad? How can we give them a heritage with firmer roots than the current peer group rage?

These are questions that go to the heart of what celebration is about. Celebration is the honoring of that which we hold most dear.

Celebration is delighting in that which tells us who we are. Celebration is taking the time to cherish each other. Celebration is returning with open arms and thankful hearts to our Maker.

In my desire to give my sons a steady place to stand, a heritage, I began looking for models, for someone who could teach me how to celebrate even in a small apartment, in urban America, in the late 20th century.

To my delight I found a community of people who have been experimenting with a variety of celebrations and traditions in just such a setting for the last 30 years. Folks here at Reba Place have worked hard to bring celebration and worship life into their home contexts. It was into their family and small-group gatherings that my quest took me. I didn't find sophistication or elaborate techniques on how best to train children according to certain developmental schemes. No. What I found were simple, unpretentious ways of celebrating life, small gestures for making family and small-group life a "means of grace", festive activities that stretch the imagination and move one toward God.

What I found here at Reba Place Church is well worth sharing. These folks have blessed me with their flair for celebration, and I hope they will bless you.

Sincerely, Sara

P.S. For more information on Reba Place Church see page 183.

Chapter One

Why Celebrate, for Heaven's Sake?

A Family-Based Revolution of Hope

What values do I hold most dear? How do I tell my children who they are and where they fit into the vast array of cultures and religions? Either I pass these values on in a haphazard fashion, or I hand them to my children like priceless heirlooms, with care and forethought. Either I take my direction from the loudest, most current voices of the mass media, or I am nurtured by centuries of traditional stories and symbols which have guided countless families in prosperity and in adversity.

Essentially we are all creatures in search of meaning, trying to make sense of the host of options that cry out to us. We can either choose to follow the trends that the dominant culture dictates, or we can select a value system informed from a treasure trove of family memories passed down through the generations.

Without a history, without a tradition on which to stand, we are shallow folk indeed.

In their family celebrations scrapbook Virgil and Joan Vogt of the Reba Place community in Chicago wrote to their daughter, "Family traditions can't be bought, no matter how wealthy we are. These treasures are acquired simply, bit by bit as time passes . . . . [They] will make for a rich family heritage, one with warm and happy memories that carry you along through good and bad times. They are worth their weight in gold!"

Handing on the Christian faith to one's children is one of the greatest privileges and most awesome responsibilities of a parent. I do it with joy and trembling. When my sons ask, "Mama, is it a risk to love God?" and "Mama, why doesn't God protect everyone who loves him?", I couldn't *begin* to formulate an answer without the stories of God's people to inform me. I need a history to get my bearings, and, even more so, to orient my sons toward the simple and profound truths of the faith. I need tried and true traditions to slow what appears to be a stampede toward high-tech titillation.

I don't want my children to become passive consumers. With a conscious effort to create or recreate family rituals, perhaps our family can join a revolt against the onslaught of depersonalizing dials and digits.

A revolution of hope will only be possible, suggests psychiatrist Erich Fromm, if we consciously seek to develop "frames of orientation and devotion." Parents must be in the vanguard of that revolution!

Children form their concepts of God long before they come into direct contact with church teaching. The role of the family in spiritual formation is normally greater than the part played by church or school. What parents hand on is not so much a received doctrine, as a *lived experience*.

Family traditions, when deliberately cultivated, build a sense of identity that will hold a family together from year to year and generation to generation. Celebrative rituals become the vehicle for passing on beliefs and values.

Rituals also provide structure in the life of a family. Admittedly, structures can be restrictive; rituals can fall into dead formality. Frameworks that no longer serve a vital purpose must be dismantled. But the solution to meaningless structure need not be a regression to chaos. Bringing order out of disorder or design out of chaos is the creative task of the artist, the Christian, and, I believe, the parent. To create a structured family environment is to fashion a rhythm of meaningful activity so that a child can know safety and true freedom.

Children need patterns and consistency in order to feel secure. There are so many changes in a child's larger world that he or she will receive great comfort from the reassuring repetition of memorable family celebrations. Children long for sameness, for the predictable return of a pleasurable experience. Like a cloak of security, repeated rituals surround a child with rhyme and reason, with anticipation and fulfillment, over and over again.

We change. We grow. We come and go. But the ritual we return to again and again enunciates that which does not change; it reaffirms those truths which provide direction in a life that is often adrift; it celebrates the eternal amid the temporal.

Sensible Bridges Into Transcendence

Religious teaching within the family is often done in a joyless context. A lack of imagination characterizes many of our family worship activities. We forget why we're doing what we're doing. The spirit evaporates. Rigor mortis sets in and family "worship," "ritual," "tradition" and "faith" all become obnoxious, boring words.

One of the best weapons we can give our children against cynicism and despair is a gift for fun. Not that all we do must be high intensity, zippy entertainment. But enjoyable? Yes. A ritual is play—

an agreed-upon pattern of meaningful, dramatized play.

Why have our religious imaginations withered? Why has worship become a dry rut instead of a wellspring of new life?

In most Protestant worship, both at home and at church, we rely heavily on the unvarnished biblical word. We lean toward a rationalist approach to religion, imagining that if we can *say* it right we'll finally get it right. We have forgotten that because human beings are a *unity* of mind, body and spirit, we need colors, candles, embraces, dances and drama to fill out our picture of truth.

Why have we forgotten? Why have we forgotten that Christian worship (as distinct from attending lectures and concerts) invites everyone to get in on the act, not as spectators, but as responsive actors? Movement is an integral part of Christian worship. Moving is essential to thinking. Ritual provides a way to harmonize our movements with their meaning.

Why have we forgotten that it is through our senses, all of them, that our hearts are enlarged so that God may enter in? The supernatural reaches us along natural paths, symbolized in the breaking of bread, the rising helium balloon on Easter morning, the hands-on parental blessing. Our senses are the vehicles through which the Spirit of God enters into our constricted thought to make space for grace.

To confine the Spirit's entering to words alone is to rob ourselves of a full-orbed worship experience. To neglect visual, tangible, symbolic "vehicles of grace" is to break a vital bridge between the heart and the Eternal.

Oh, for the ability to approach God with our entire being, rather than fixating only on talk *about* God!

Why have we forgotten? The wordy austerity of much contemporary worship life stems in part from the time of the Protestant Reformation. During the 16th century, Protestant reformers ruthlessly condemned external symbols of religiosity such as the Roman Catholic liturgy, vestments, pictures, candles, incense, crosses, organs and processions. John Calvin, a Swiss reformer, felt that ceremonious religion presented an obstacle to true worship and that attention should focus instead on one God who is Spirit. Since God's self is revealed to us in the Bible, in language, the Puritan reformers felt that it is through words alone that we should pray to and adore God.

The reformers saw correctly, I think, that external ceremonious religion is inadequate and, in extreme cases, magical. A heavy dependence on ceremony can easily slide into crass materialism. The fire of reform did burn up a lot of fluff. Yet that same fire left us with little, other than words, for grasping the intimate relatedness of our humanity and God's transcendence.

We are essentially beings who, while concretely anchoring ourselves in our world, seek to transcend ourselves and our world. When we are discouraged or lonely we turn to music, or to painting, to prayer or to the Eucharist, and "as compensation beyond all price," Madeleine L'Engle writes, "we are given glimpses of the world on the other side of time and space."

Through our senses we are able to reach out toward the supra-sensible. This is a deep mystery! Concrete symbols and ritual play connect us somehow with the eternal, the incomprehensible. And too, they are especially appropriate for children because many of them don't require a certain level of knowledge before one can participate. They make tangible for children what is intangible. They convey a simple, elementary meaning that can grow with us as we grow in our ability to comprehend.

Family worship rituals lead us toward an *experience* of the mystery of God's transcendence which, in our efforts to *explain* God, we have neglected to our own detriment. We are led to pray, "Enlarge our hearts, Oh Lord, that you may enter in."

And too, family worship rituals celebrate the incarnation—God with us. It was Christ who drew from the ordinary things of life to point to the reality of God in our midst: a farmer planting seed, a woman's use of yeast in baking, the relationship of a father and two sons. By God's grace the common stuff of life becomes sacred, leading us toward God.

Stories—The Staff of Life

"Nothing is as strong to save us as a STORY," asserts Madeleine L'Engle, a storyteller par excellence. "Jesus was not a theologian," she continues. "He was God who told stories."

Children love to hear stories about when their parents were little and stories about grandparents and great-grandparents. Stories about where we as a people have come from help us to understand why we are where we are right now. Stories give us a sense of continuity, of belonging to a river of life.

Parent storytellers make conscious those things which are not seen by the child, but which tell the child what part he or she plays in an immense drama that extends through the ages. To tell the stories that come from the Judeo-Christian tradition and to enrich them from other traditions is to invite children into a drama with cosmic dimensions, and yet one in which each child has a unique part to play.

Through stories an individual life is related to the overarching meaning of the cosmos; each individual story is linked with a Great Story.

Story is a way of dealing with the confusion and terror that confront every child at some time or other. The more stories of goodness and courage a child knows, the more fortified he or she is for dealing with the reality of evil. Such stories give hope and affirm that love is stronger than hate. Stories that tell of individuals whose love endured and whose hope refused to be quenched describe the working of a greater Love, the love of God which endures forever.

Family rituals on religious holidays, at bedtimes or at major times of transition, like weddings and funerals, are powerful primarily because they provide the opportunity to tell the familiar stories again and again.

Family worship rituals invite us to re-create God's redemptive actions revealed in history so that our *now* is caught up with the stories of God's past faithfulness and moved toward God's future.

The Jewish Bedrock of Family Celebrations

Jewish festive traditions are especially well adapted for telling and retelling the faith story. The primary action on a Jewish holiday is usually within the home rather than in the synagogue. Jewish people have a long tradition of sustaining a family-centered worship life from which Christians can learn a lot.

Jewish liturgy and festivals are the source of much of our Christian worship life. Many Jewish celebrations honor a history which we share. The source of their story is also the source of our story. Participation in their festive reenactments of that story brings us closer to our own cultural and historical roots.

The Jews gave us Christ. The prayers, readings, blessings and symbols that Christ used grew out of a thoroughly Jewish context. Christian interpretation of these symbols doesn't so much change the Jewish symbols as it adds a new layer of meaning to them. The meaning of Jewish symbols such as fire, water, paschal lamb and unleavened bread is focused in Christian practice, not negated or

11

obliterated. Understanding the original Jewish meaning of the symbols can restore an historical foundation to our Christian interpretations.

John and Sharie Habegger of Reba Place explain why their family celebrates Jewish holidays:

> Our involvement and participation in the Jewish festival calendar has been a central part of our married life. We both come from "low church" backgrounds which shied away from ritual as an expression of our Christian faith. One of the main attractions of the Jewish festivals is the rootedness they offer in understanding who Jesus was in his human form, and the expression of God's faithfulness to this people of faith.
>
> While it is sometimes difficult for us to juggle all of the scheduling necessary to celebrate Passover and Channukah along with Easter and Christmas, we experience a sense of wholeness and completeness that is precious.

It is especially the home-centered quality of the Jewish festivals that makes them well suited to enrich our family rituals. Because celebrations happen at home, they have been adapted to include children. The ceremonies for Sabbath and the the Passover, for example, are filled with poetic symbols which embrace the mental, the spiritual and the physical. Jewish art and history are woven into the fabric of each festival. For those who can't read, there are bitter herbs to taste and candles to light as a way of entering into the experience.

The festivals often occur around the dinner table where eating and enjoyment of special foods become an important part of the larger commemorative worship drama. Simply by being present at the festive dinner table, a child is introduced to the noblest treasures of the faith. As the drama of lights, readings and symbols unfolds, the child is drawn into profound reenactment of faith tradition. Whether or not the child is aware, he or she is being given a place of belonging, a steady foundation on which to stand. And what more valuable gift can we give to our children?

Play Rehearsal for the Future

Worship rituals, while undergirding a family with a bedrock of memory, don't abandon us to wander in the past. Rather, they thrust us, with renewed hope, into the future. When our memory of God's faithfulness is revived, we can make bold to venture into unfamiliar territory.

The times in which we live are fraught with fear about the future. Grounds for hope can quickly erode when confronted with the objective reality of our contemporary world.

Family rituals are a mainstay against the encroachment of despair. Hopeful people both discover and express their faith in God's future through rituals and celebrations. Someone has asked, "Is it too much to hope that by acting like we are at a heavenly banquet we may hasten its coming and our own entrance into that Kingdom which comes so highly recommended to children?"

By playfully entering into celebration we rehearse for the future. It's as though we play an "eschatological game," believing that the grand fulfillment which will come can be envisioned and rehearsed now. The joy of clasping hands around the table, of singing the "songs of Zion" to the beat of the children's rhythm instruments, of "passing the peace"—the celebration of the presence of the Kingdom *now* makes us receptive also to as-yet-unrealized possibilities in the future.

Family worship is not usually the socially accepted thing to do. To choose to worship is to choose a nonconformist stance toward life. It is to choose a radically different way of being. In worship, we open ourselves to change; we make ourselves vulnerable to heart-wrenching conviction and painful, but joyful, new beginnings. In worship we expect our eyes to be opened so that we will recognize "the Risen Lord in the breaking of the bread."

In worship we expect to move and be moved, to touch and be touched. Worship disturbs us and energizes us for action. By experiencing a foretaste of what God has in store for God's people, we grow restless with the status quo.

The vision of a world of unbounded realities stays with us throughout the mundane work of day upon day. The prayer "Thy Kingdom come" gives us eyes to see hints of its presence everywhere.

Chapter Two

Daily Spirituality and Rituals

Mundane Rhythms and Sacred Rhymes

The sun rises at the beginning of a new day. The night's sleep has been shallow, punctuated by a child's coughing. Now there are lunches to pack, a sick child to comfort, a lost boot to search for, and a general rush to get everyone moving in one direction or another. Will this be one more day where countless tasks fragment my sense of well-being? From where can I find the stamina to meet the challenges this day, and every day?

The question is a monumental one, particularly for those who seek to live a godly life. Where can ordinary folk find a theology which springs from our everyday tasks and returns to invigorate us right where we are? My sense is that either faith must give me food for the road on a blurred, beleaguered morning, or it might as well (regardless of whether it came from fathers or mothers, theologians or preachers) be stashed between two gilded book covers and set on a museum shelf to molder.

If it isn't possible to know the quickening presence of God in the everyday routine, one might as well ship religiosity off to a seminary library and leave it there. Either God is the God of all life, or God is on the reserve shelf, available and relevant only to a sanctified elite.

Present In the Practical

I want to breathe in fresh air, bandage a bleeding knee, pick up trash around the neighborhood, cook a meal and know that what I do is all done for the love of God.

Our favorite distinctions between sacred and secular are generally unhelpful. We cannot divide the spiritual from the practical. We are amphibious beings, creatures of spirit and of sense. It is through all the circumstances, inward and outward, that we are fed supernatural food.

Jesus conveyed better than anyone that spirituality is inextricably woven into the stuff of daily life. He longed to gather Jerusalem's children as a hen gathers her chicks under her wings; he likened God to a diligent woman who sweeps her house in search of one lost coin, to the lighting of lamps, the use of preservative salt, the removing of a splinter in the eye, the building of a house. Jesus' teaching is filled with homey, down-to-earth realities. The ordinary things of life provide the material for God's redeeming action.

Learning how to cultivate the presence of God throughout our daily activities can be a revolutionary discovery. Prayer doesn't need to be a formal, lengthy exercise that one only gets around to now and then. Instead, prayer can be like breathing, like continually feeling loved by God. With a little discipline we can learn to offer our activities, small and large, to God, doing what we would normally do, but doing it for the love of God.

As we do for God's sake what we normally do for ourselves, each deed, no matter how mundane, can become an act of worship. When prayer accompanies all that we do, our whole life becomes an offering of prayer.

Wondering Into Mystery

Opening oneself to wonder, to delight, is one of the best ways I know of cultivating the presence of God. Without the ability to wonder, all things become commonplace. But, when we open ourselves to wonder, everything is potentially sacramental.

More than likely our children will awaken us to wonder. As parents we may think a quiet stroll on the beach would be nice, but our children call us to activity—gathering shells, yelling into the wind, making footprint designs in the sand. By entering into those experiences with abandon we stay in touch with celebration, with worship.

From the microscopic picture of the crystalline structure of a snowflake to the clusters and superclusters of galaxies, each with hundreds of billions of stars, it seems our world is designed to confound us, to stagger the imagination. After centuries of study, astronomers and physicists have more questions than answers.

Entering into awe with one's child is a delightful way of introducing a child to God. In any one of our days there is enough all around us to "trigger a revelation," a peek into the incomprehensible beauty of God. A cup of milk, a flexing elbow, a thundercloud—each is a potential pathway to God. Being alive to the world nurtures a spirit of worship. By entering into the mystery of "how could this be," we embark on an adventure along a wonder-strewn pathway toward infinity.

Wondering Into Prayer

Nurturing wonder goes hand in hand with learning to give

thanks. We have no better defense against pessimism and despair than one simple virtue—the ability to delight in life no matter what it brings. Gratitude makes us receptive to God's action in our lives as little else can.

And our children learn from our ability to give thanks that, truly, there is nothing that can separate us from the love of God. That is why we celebrate, even when all is not well; that is why we delight in a juicy red apple even while grieving in the knowledge that others are starving. Not that we are any more deserving, but the apple *has* been given and we rejoice. The Giver of all good would want us to rejoice. Rather than taking the Creator's provision for granted, when we celebrate the goodness of the gift we increase the possibility that the realm of goodness will be enlarged.

When we cultivate a spirit of thankfulness, we find God in the small actions and things around us. Prayer with a child before meals or at bedtime is an appropriate time to mention particular objects and feelings that are immediately knowable to the child. Rather than using pious phrases that are meaningless to him or her we can notice what is on the table, remark on the weather outside, remember an event from the child's day and lift up these in gratitude. A mealtime prayer by one of our sons not long ago illustrates the point: "Thank you for the yummy spaghetti, the cold water, the broccoli; thank you for the good food in the whole world; please don't let yourself die and don't let Mommy die. Amen."

Many a night at bedtime our youngest will simply pray, "Watch over me tonight. Amen." But other times when the spirit so moves, he will launch into his own unique prayer, like the night he repeatedly jumped into bed: "God, thank you for my nice bed that I could go splat in. Thank you that I'm alive. Thank you for fresh air. Thank you for the world. Amen."

It is through the particular, not through vague generalities, that we come closest to our own sensuous humanity, to the humanity we share with others, and to God. The Creator's obvious attention to infinitesimal detail in constructing our world warrants our notice, our praise, our celebration.

It is also in the particular action that our children learn what it is to care for others. Endless talk about widespread injustice is not as likely to motivate compassion as one encounter with a needy individual. We learn of Jesus' love by the way he *acted* toward a woman accused of adultery, and by the way he welcomed the children onto his lap. Had he merely expounded on the virtues of forgiveness or of childlikeness without exemplifying them in specific action, his impact would have been minimal.

It is specific acts of kindness and courtesy sprinkled throughout the day that make all the difference between a family that slowly disintegrates and a family that, against all odds, grows in harmony.

Cutting Familiar Paths

The spirituality of the family must be nurtured daily. Simple daily rituals can fortify us to handle the daily demands. There is abundant joy and inner quietude available for the person willing to exert a little effort each day to be with God.

Establishing a pattern to our seeking is rather like cutting paths through the underbrush on our way through the forest to the river. We can fight our way through the underbrush to arrive infrequently at the river, or we can cut paths which lead us with relative ease to the river for refreshment, cleansing and recreation.

Daily Rituals, from Sunrise to Sunset

Daily spirituality can be enhanced by a variety of individual and family activities. One doesn't need many such activities to bring order and joy to the day. Spirituality isn't helped by overdoing rituals with the idea that the more one does, the more religious one becomes. Rather, one can select several activities that best suit one's style and pace. Families where both parents work outside the home know—or will discover—that giving meaningful time to one or two activities can be far more uplifting than racing compulsively through the whole gamut of possibilities.

I have selected some examples of activities that Reba Place folks enjoy, hoping that they may serve to spark other individuals and families to actively cultivate a sense of God's presence. Clearly, one must slow down enough to preserve time for worship, to make space for grace.

Breakfast Traditions

Breakfast with adults and children sitting together around the table has been a frequent practice in many Reba Place homes. A short devotional time preceding the meal often includes a song and scripture reading. Conversation then centers on the prospects for the day, and special prayer is offered for any concerns that children or adults may raise.

1. A Traditional Song to Greet the Morning

A traditional song to greet the morning at Reba Place breakfast tables is "Each Morning Brings."

Each Morning Brings

Johannes Zwick, 1496-1542
Tr. Margaret Barclay, 1951

ALL MORGEN IST L.M.
Melody, Wittenberg, 1537

1. Each morn-ing brings us fresh out-poured, The lov-ing-kind-ness of the Lord.
2. All darkness in us Lord dispell, From bitterness O shield us well.
3. O God, thou star of dawn-ing day Give us that light for which we pray;

It ends not as the day goes past, But gives us strength while life shall last.
From ill desires, from clouded sight, O do thou lead us day and night.
Make thou thy flame in us to glow, That we no lack of grace may know.

From *The Pilgrim Hymnal,* © 1931, 35, 58 by The Pilgrim Press Used by permission.

2. A Morning Prayer

The printed morning prayer included below is adapted from an unknown source. It has been used during morning devotionals in several Reba Place homes and serves to illustrate how printed prayers can be used instead of or to supplement spontaneous prayers around the breakfast table. Or, a family member may want to write a family prayer that celebrates a particular family event and serves to commemorate God's faithfulness each morning it is read.

Spirit of the Living God,

By faith I acknowledge with thanksgiving
Your presence in me.
You have made your home
In the depths of my being;
Deeper than my thoughts,
My feelings, my will.
I praise you,
I worship you,
I love you,
I thank you
For descending to such depths
So you could dwell in my body,
Making it your temple.
Above all,
I thank you for revealing to me
The Lord Jesus Christ, my Saviour,
And for giving to me
All the blessings of His life and death.

At the beginning of this new day
I want to yield myself
Wholly and completely
To your will and leading.
Guide me,
And prepare me for each occasion
To experience your mighty power.
Give me an opportunity today
To renounce and put to death self,

So Jesus Christ can live in me.
Make me a channel of love and healing,
Power and blessing
To any you bring across my path
And want me to meet today.
Holy Spirit, I pray that all may be done
To the glory of our loving Father in heaven,
And may He be pleased with me today. Amen.

3. One Family's Breakfast Worship Ritual

Cindy and Tom Taylor have four children, aged 9-15. They have recently begun a family breakfast activity which promises to become a tradition. The family gathers for breakfast at 7:00 a.m. After a light meal, each member of the family is responsible, on a rotating basis, to give leadership to a short devotional time. Nine-year-old Naomi usually reads from her Bible Story book. The teens may have a scripture reading, usually accompanied by some probing questions. Mom or Dad may offer a short teaching on a scripture. Rotating the responsibility gives each child the opportunity to exercise leadership and to bring his or her special interests to the family. The children are glad to participate if they are encouraged, Cindy observed. They are learning to support and be considerate of each other's efforts. Usually the devotional time includes a song and ends with prayer. Each family member mentions a prayer concern and then each prays for the person to his or her left, going around the table.

4. Note Cards at the Breakfast Table

An occasional breakfast table tradition described by Sara Ewing includes note cards set at each plate which have been prepared by mother, father, child or housemate. The words on the outside of the note cards are the same for each individual. They may be: "The Lord is...", or, "Redemption comes through...", or, "I am saved from..." On opening the card, each individual finds a different completion to the opening phrase—a personal word to carry throughout the day: "The Lord is—your Shepherd. You need not be anxious about anything." Or, "The Lord is—the light of your morning and will go with you on your way."

Each person then reads his or her personal word to the others.

5. Hands-On Parental Blessings

The whole concept of blessing is an important one that we have too often disregarded, remarks Virgil Vogt. Godly people have the power to convey a blessing, he reflects. Blessing someone doesn't just mean giving a nice word or engaging in wishful thinking. Rather, it is an empowering, conveyed by the laying on of hands, a parent to a child, or a friend to a friend.

When people brought children to Jesus so that he might touch them, he "took the children in his arms, put his hands on them and blessed them" (Mk. 10:13). Most of us have usually confined the laying on of hands to churchly functions like ordination, yet the opportunity to bless our children is with us every day—as they go to school, or to bed or whenever. "May the Lord bless you and keep you. May the Lord be gracious to you and give you peace. Amen."

6. Lunch Box Surprises

A daily ritual at the Shuford home for several years was to write a note to be included in each child's lunch box. Lois and Bob wrote these lunch box notes especially in the years that their children were adapting to school life. The notes were meant to reassure the children that parental care didn't stop when they were absent from each other. A humorous rhyme or a loving thought on paper served to remind the child at lunch time that he or she was not forgotten. To illustrate, a few lines might say:

> While you munch
> This yummy lunch
> Know that we love you
> A great big bunch.

At the early stage in their family life when Lois had to leave for work before her little daughter was awake, Lois always left Becky a note on the breakfast table that Bob could read to her to remind her of her mother's care. Now, as the children grow older and go separate ways, each leaves notes on the table for other family members indicating where the writer has gone and when he or she will return. Notes provide a way for family members to show that they matter to one another, even while going many different ways.

7. Lunch Box Notes

Cindy and Tom Taylor's children, even as they enter the teen years, have requested that their mother continue a lunch-box-note ritual which has gone on for several years. Every morning, Cindy takes a square piece of paper or a note card, puts a sticker on each and writes a scripture verse for each child. A note goes into each lunch box. Recently, Cindy has been searching particularly for verses about children. She uses the concordance a lot, gathering verses over a period of time that relate to a common theme. When her children were complaining about having trouble falling asleep, Cindy found verses pertinent to that theme, used them in lunch boxes and in making posters for the children's bedrooms. "When you apply the Bible to life," Cindy said, "it becomes a more positive thing than when the Bible is just something Mom and Dad do."

8. A Tasty Treat

Brigitte Krummel, whose daughters are now both in college, remembers that every day when she made the lunches for her children she added something special—a dessert or treat—that they didn't expect. The extra effort it took to include an element of surprise served symbolically as a reminder, in much the same way as a note, that the parent had put forth an effort beyond the call of duty to remember and love her child even when they weren't together. The effort on the parent's part is minimal compared with the well-being borne out in the child.

9. Making Good Use of Teachable Moments

Bob and Lois Shuford talk about being alert to the teachable moments throughout a day. Though not exactly a ritual, this attitude readies one to respond on the spur of the moment when a child's curiosity makes him or her more open to learning than perhaps during the regularly prescribed slots for learning.

An example from the Shenk home to illustrate a teachable moment: I remember one day when Joseph felt he just *had* to hear and see Jesus. He wanted with his whole being to experience Jesus in a tangible, first-hand way. I was at a loss as to what to do since my explanations wouldn't satisfy his desire. Then an idea occurred to me. I suggested that we read the story of St. Francis of Assisi, a person who wanted above all to be with Jesus. Joseph said he'd like to read it together. It was the right thing to do; an unplanned worship experience for us both in the middle of the day. A supply of short biographical stories on one's bookshelf, about remarkable people, can be an invaluable resource for teachable moments.

10. Thank-You Board

Neta Jackson describes one tradition that she has seen in several homes around Reba Place: A Thank-You Board. The concept is simple. One needs only a blank sheet of paper pinned up in a central location, on a bulletin board or refrigerator, with a pen or marker readily accessible nearby. The idea is that anytime someone feels thankful for something another member of the household did, like remembering to take the garbage out, or making a bed, or cooking a special dish for dinner, or whatever, he or she writes a little message to that person. Often when it occurs to us to thank someone, that person has already gone to work or to bed. The Thank-You Board provides a means to relate our thanks when we've failed to give the more immediate, verbal appreciation or when we just want to make a tiny public monument to someone we love, perhaps even to God. When the paper gets filled, one simply removes it and starts again with a fresh piece of paper.

11. "Glad to Be Home"

Kay Holler relates a daily ritual that her husband, Steve, initiated in their home, a ritual which seems small but is large with significance. "Every evening since we've been married, Steve comes home from work and shouts from the front door, 'The luckiest man in the world is home!' I've been hearing this for two and a half years now," writes Kay, "and it still makes me feel good."

And another interesting ritual in the Holler home is that Steve makes a pie (all different kinds) every 13th of the month to make a "superstitiously bad day into a good one."

Mealtime Rituals

Mealtimes are given great prominence in many Reba Place homes. "We give priority to daily mealtimes," remarks Virgil Vogt, "because they are foundational to family life."

Mealtimes, and especially the evening dinner, are a symbolic act, a deliberate ritual of human interaction that embodies the best of what life has to offer: good food which is necessary for physical well-being and good fellowship which enhances spiritual well-being. Jesus often talked about "sitting at table." The ritual of sharing food together colors many of his parables about banquets and wedding feasts. Feasting at table depicts the longed-for presence of the Kingdom of God more powerfully than any other conceivable symbol. The intimate statement in Revelation 3:20 beautifully sums up God's aspirations for us, and I believe, ours for God: "Here I am! I stand at the door and knock. If anyone hears my voice and opens the door, I will go in and *eat with him [her], and he [she] with me.*"

Besides the obvious features of a family dinner, such as all sitting down together to share food, there are special features which folks at Reba Place use to "spice up" the meal.

12. One Favorite Original Table Grace

Though a family may enjoy singing a variety of different songs before meals, one favorite table grace which Joanna and John Lehman say they have often used in their home is a thanksgiving round, composed by a long-time member of Reba Place.

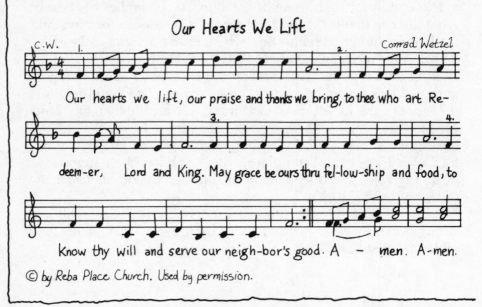

Our Hearts We Lift

C.W.   Conrad Wetzel

Our hearts we lift, our praise and thanks we bring, to thee who art Re-

deem-er, Lord and King. May grace be ours thru fel-low-ship and food, to

know thy will and serve our neigh-bor's good. A — men. A-men.

© by Reba Place Church. Used by permission.

13. Dressing Up the Dinner Table

Neta Jackson tells how she likes to dress up the dinner table with candles and with their nice set of dishes. Just a touch of formality contributes to the sense that mealtimes are special family times.

A single rosebud or one candle, when provided with thoughtfulness can be more meaningful than a lavish centerpiece (not to mention the ease and greater frequency with which one can afford to add such simple grace notes to a meal). Nor is it usually a fantastic spread of different foods that does the most for strengthening family bonds. A simple meal, that didn't take too much out of the cook to prepare, and a welcome-to-the-table hug will go farther toward nourishing meaningful family relationships than an opulent spread.

14. Prayer File Box for Mealtime

For their table grace, the Jackson family makes use of a prayer file box filled with note cards on which, over the months, they have written numerous prayer requests. Before the prayer, they take out one card and include that request in their table grace. The card is then placed at the back of the file. Depending on the number of prayer requests, it will reappear at the front again in several weeks. If there has been an answer to prayer, this will be noted on the card. If someone has a new request, a new card will be added to the file. The card collection gives significant direction and continuity to their family prayer life, providing them with an opportunity to celebrate resolutions to problems and to join together with ongoing concerns.

15. Joining Hands for Table Grace

The Shufords always join hands around the table as the grace is said. Besides the sense of unity it gives to the family circle, it also makes it easier to quiet any small child that has a propensity to fidget during the prayer or song.

When the meal is brought on in the Shuford home, before the food is even tasted, everyone gives a "Hand for the cook." The round of applause isn't appraisal of the cook's success or lack of it, but a gesture of appreciation for his or her good efforts.

16. Reading Scriptures at Table

Vera Stoehr remembers reading scriptures at every meal in her Jewish Christian childhood home. Verses were read around the table with the older children joining in as their reading skills grew. Vera says that her parents successfully communicated their warmth and love for the Scripture, which was the key to making this daily ritual a satisfying one even for the children, one that Vera recalls with great fondness.

17. Traditional Jewish After-Meal Blessing

A short blessing recited after the meal could become a simple but precious family ritual. A traditional Jewish blessing partially included below, which dates back to before Jesus' time, is an example of a prayer from which an individual family could adapt its own short after-meal blessing.*

You are blessed, Lord our God,
   King of the universe,
you who nourish the entire world
with goodness, tender love, and mercy.
   You are blessed, O Lord,
you who nourish the universe.

We will give you thanks, Lord our God,
for you have given us a desirable land for our inheritance,
that we may eat of its fruits
and be filled with its goodness.
You are blessed, Lord our God,
for the land and the food.

You are blessed, Lord our God,
   King of the universe,
you who are good and filled with kindness!
You are blessed, Lord our God,
   King of the universe,
you who are good and filled with kindness!

* Note: *Efforts have been made throughout the book to use inclusive language about God and humans. Language about God and men and women is too important to be trapped in traditional usage alone. However, the author also feels that traditional and biblical poetry and phraseology often cannot be altered without damaging the literary and historical integrity of the text. Consequently the reader will find most traditional Jewish expressions and scriptural quotations throughout the book basically unaltered. Those who are seeking to grow in sensitivity to inclusive language are encouraged to refer to the* Inclusive Language Lectionary *noted on page 187 for alternative scripture readings, or to substitute names for God which more adequately reflect their own relationship with the Holy One.*

18. Adapting When the Time Comes

Dave Jackson explains how his and Neta's family's devotional activities have evolved over the years in response to the changing interests of their two children:

"Family devotions have always been challenging for us but we keep looking for new, creative ways that will make them work. We've discovered over the years that when the children lose interest in a particular family activity, rather than leaning on them to keep participating or pumping more energy into the event, we parents need to adapt our activities to stimulate new interest.

"When our children were little we could read them almost anything geared to their age and hold their attention, so Bible stories worked well. But our children are six years apart, and our son Julian, our oldest, began to grow out of that.

"In addition, summertime poses a problem. It is hard to keep any kid's attention when there are several hours of daylight after dinner that beckon him or her to go out to play. Family worship activities that compete with time the children would much rather be using for other things, are sure to create tension and lack of enthusiasm.

"A prayer box, which Neta described earlier, was one solution we have used off and on with fair success. It was exciting to make the rounds on the cards and realize that God had frequently answered the prayer, so we'd thank God and add a new card. The prayer file box provides us with a simple, unobtrusive way to integrate worship into our family rhythm.

"Another solution that worked fairly well when Julian was in eighth and ninth grades and Rachel was in third and fourth was doing a Bible study on Christian character traits. We used the guide, *Building Christian Character*, published by Bethany House Publishers. Each week we would begin by mentioning the theme and learning a verse for that week, usually practiced at breakfast. Then on Wednesday evening we would take a longer devotional time—maybe a half hour or 40 minutes—and talk about the subject, ask questions and read any reflections from the study guide.

"That seemed to work for awhile, but then Julian's life became more congested with an evening job, dating and with special events at the high school or church, and we couldn't be sure of evening schedules.

"We had to find another alternative. One that seems to be working now is for Neta and me to take turns each week reading a dozen or so verses from the Bible at breakfast. As much as possible, we try to follow themes that last about a week and arise from questions or comments the kids mention. For instance, one day Julian made a comment that he wasn't really sure that the Bible said there was a hell. So, for the next week we read passages relevant to this question: we titled it, 'A Heaven to Be Gained, and a Hell to Be Shunned.' On another occasion, Rachel raised a question about what exactly was involved in becoming a Christian, so we took a couple weeks to read all the stories of or messages about conversion in the New Testament, reading one each morning. We identified the common themes and also the variations in the ways people came to Christ.

"One reason for using breakfast is that there's nothing competing for the kids' interest. It takes about 15 minutes to eat, and usually friends, TV and the activities of the day haven't yet caught their attention. They may be a little groggy, but there seems to be more response.

"I'm sure the time will soon come when we have to come up with another approach.

"Our consistency in having family devotions comes and goes, usually in this fashion: We make a valiant start on a new plan and it works well for awhile. Then it gets interrupted for some legitimate reasons. We gear up and make another try, but, after awhile, that fizzles and we go for weeks with nothing until Neta and I sit down and admit that the last approach is no longer working. We've found that as the kids grow and change, what works at one stage just can't be forced in another. We don't feel we have to entertain our children for devotions. On the other hand, a primary object for us is to avoid making listening to the Lord a miserable experience. So we're always looking for something new that may fit our family's next stage."

After-Dinner Traditions

19. Family Read-Aloud Time

Following the evening meal at the Jackson home, everyone goes to the living room for a half hour of reading aloud. Even though the Jackson children, aged 10 and 16, read books on their own, the tradition of Dad or Mom reading a favorite book aloud to the whole family has become a cherished one. When the children were younger, reading stories happened one on one at bedtime. But as the children went to bed later and later and outgrew bedtime stories, sharing books together as a foursome after dinner has become the family pattern. Classics which the family has enjoyed, to name a few, are *The Narnia Chronicles*, the *Little House* books, *The Wind in the Willows*, *Old Yeller*, *Rascal* and many more.

20. Making Reading Attractive for the Family

The joy of regularly sharing a good book, whether at bedtime or anytime, provides an excellent way for *really* beginning to think together about ideas as parent and child. Parents who make reading as a family attractive are laying an essential foundation at an early age for good communication between the generations later on. Sharing the pleasure of well-chosen words, the emotions of fear and joy, and the mind-expanding fun of great ideas is one of the most rewarding family recreations! The more shared adventures in reading a family has, the better they will understand and enjoy each other.

21. Memorizing Verse as a Family

Children can also be taught to memorize poetry and scripture during the family reading time. Rote memorization for any reason *other* than the fun of hearing the music, rhythm and beauty of good verse is apt to kill the desire to memorize. One significant way to encourage the desire is for the parents to enter into the experience themselves, demonstrating that memorization can be fun.

If we come to the reading or memorization of scripture, or any family ritual for that matter, with a sense of obligation instead of enjoyment, or with the idea that this is the time for religious indoctrination instead of a time for exploring truth, we will ruin it for our children. If we haven't compartmentalized religion into one little family-devotions slot but let faith inform all of life, we'll find many of our children joining in the adventure wholeheartedly.

22. After-Dinner Hymn-Sing with Children's Rhythm Instruments

Nearly every evening after dinner the Vogt family sings hymns around the piano. Young children can join in family sing-alongs with a variety of rhythm instruments like small bells, sticks or tambourines. Keeping a basket of instruments readily available by the piano provides a delightful incentive for all ages to contribute to a festive family sing-along.

23. A Good Old-Fashioned Walk

The Shenk family began an after-dinner ritual not long ago which promises to become a regular when the weather invites: a good, old-fashioned walk. It requires no preparation ahead of time and no cleaning up afterwards. Yet the satisfaction it brings is hard to match—and at such a sane pace! We pass many joggers and dog-walkers but very, very seldom a family all together. The walk, usually no more than a half-hour long, allows us to talk, observe the clouds and setting sun, watch the birds, collect leaves and other "finds," play tag. After filling our lungs with plenty of fresh air, it's back home for dishes and bedtime stories.

24. Evening Prayer Time

The Roddy family used to have a time of evening prayer before going to bed, with the parents and four or five of the older children participating. Though the children are grown now and many have their own families, son Matthew remembers this ritual as an especially meaningful one. While kneeling together in a circle in the living room, the family responsively recited Psalms and prayers together using small booklets prepared for such an occasion. One could quite readily adapt prayers or Psalms from other prayer books or from scripture itself for responsive family reading.

Matthew noted that especially during the teen years, when young people may find it difficult to join in spontaneous prayer, participation in a more structured printed prayer is often easier and more appropriate. The Roddy family evening prayer lasted no more than ten minutes. It provided a brief and peaceful closure to the day.

Bedtime Rituals

At bedtime it seems that a child often asks, in a variety of ways, the metaphysical question, "Is everything alright?" As the night creeps in, fears of darkness and aloneness surface. A message of comfort from parent to child in the evening hours is extremely important. Bedtime is the time a parent can communicate reassurance ritually, by reenacting actions and words each night that say, "Yes, I am with you. You are safe, and yes, everything *is* alright."

25. Bedtime "Whispers"

Bob Shuford writes about bedtime at their home: "When Gabe and Jessy were about two and three, I started doing bedtime 'whispers' (the last thing before lights out) and have been doing them with our three younger ones ever since. 'Whispers' are messages of love I whisper in each ear, usually a simple poem I make up at the time, like 'Roses are red, violets are blue, don't you know, God loves you.' They get more ambitious at times, and go off into free verse, or sometimes I get stuck without a rhyme and we both burst out laughing. Gabe likes to give me ratings, as in a gymnastics routine, with scores ranging from a perfect 10 to a 4—(sorry Dad!). Whispering directly in someone's ear has a kind of intimacy and closeness to it; that's what prompted me to start. Gabe is eleven now and still doesn't want to stop."

26. Silent Prayer at Bedtime

Another Shuford idea is silent prayer at bedtime. Bob writes: "Once in a while I will ask the children to pray silently instead of out loud. After finishing, I ask them what they prayed, and they tell me. Then I pray silently; they ask me what I prayed, and I tell them. I started doing this to make the point that they are praying to God, not to me or for me."

27. "Bad Dream Chaser"

Lois Shuford says that a "bad dream chaser" resides at their home. An old, worn teddy bear that used to belong to Mom when she was little becomes the close companion of any child who is especially afraid or has trouble going to sleep on a particular night.

28. Finishing Unfinished Business

Neta Jackson told how bedtime at their home is a long, leisurely resolution to the day. When the children were small, there were stories and songs at bedtime, but now the focus is more on conversation at bedside about any unfinished business that may remain from the day. Parent and child will then pray together, clasping each other's hands. Frequently both parents will come to a child's bedside to chat and bid good-night.

29. Reading and Playing in Bed

Brigitte Krummel recalls that her daughters went to bed early in the evening and then, with lights on, read or played quietly in bed for as long as they wanted. The stipulations—"quiet and in bed"— were important because after a busy day of interaction with her daughters, Brigitte felt the need for personal quiet space in the evening. When she tucked her daughters in, Brigitte talked and prayed with them, and always sang. She usually sang one of five favorite bedtime songs so that her daughters could sing along. And then there was plenty of glorious time to read in bed.

30. Making Bedtime Fun

When John and Joanna Lehman's three children were young, the accent on bedtime rituals was to make them fun. John and Joanna were aware that the transition from a half hour of stories to actually getting the children into bed is often a difficult and teary one. To fill the gap, Mom and Dad ran upstairs and downstairs with the kids acting out Wee Willy Winky, and finally, at the dramatic climax, popped them into bed with a laugh.

Then after a little quiet time with each child at bedside came a final good-night song. Without the song the children never quite felt their going to bed was complete.

All Night

Refrain: All night all night the angels are watching o'er me

All night all night the angels are watching o'er me

Verse: 'now I lay me down to sleep, the angel are watching o'er me
(repeat refrain)

I pray thee Lord my soul to keep, the angels are watching o'er me.

Chapter Three
Weekly Rhythms

Spirituality in Seven Day Cycles

The sun is no respecter of the days of the week—it comes up on Monday the same as on Saturday. Our rising from bed on Saturday, however, is accompanied by a (generally acknowledged) vastly different set of feelings than our rising on Monday. We feel differently about weekends than about week days, even though the recurring weekends have nothing whatever to do with the sun or the seasons.

Weekend and work-day segments are a human construction—a rhythm of beginnings and endings that have become essential to our ability to cope with the march of time. Without the anticipated return of the weekend, the unending progression of days would look wearisome indeed. Especially since industrialization and urbanization, when the vast majority of us are separated from any real dependence on seedtime and harvest, have we needed to latch onto a predictable pattern of pacing our lives.

We need a rhythm that includes work and relaxation. Repetition of similar patterns week after week reassures us. Especially to children, the repetition of a predictable routine speaks of continuity, of order, of security.

A Sabbath Day "Bit of Nothing"

Weekends are a human construction, I said. Well, not entirely. It does seem that we were nudged in the direction of week-long segments by an all-wise God, who, knowing our inclination toward frenzied lifestyles said, "Remember the Sabbath day by keeping it holy. Six days you shall labor and do all your work, but the seventh is a Sabbath to the Lord your God. On it you shall not do any work.... For in six days the Lord made the heavens and the earth, the sea, and all that is in them. But he rested on the seventh day" (Ex. 20:8–11). Civilized society went one step further, saying that persons should have two days in which to plan their own time for work at home or for rest.

Why is it that in contemporary society we are finding it so hard to "drop out" for even one day? The Old Testament's humane commandment gives us religious license to do nothing but *rest* on one day of the week. Yet most of us work five days at one job and proceed to work two days at another.

Has the traditionally sacred space on Sundays now become a catchall day for unfinished errands and leftover tasks because life in general is more frantic than it used to be? Our week-at-a-glance calendars no longer have space for "a bit of nothing." We schedule work, friendship and family into split-second sequences throughout all the days. When the church no longer dares to tell us that Sunday is a sacred day, we appear to lack the discipline ourselves to reserve it for rest. With our freedom to make of Sundays what we individually will, we appear to be *losing* the freedom to rest.

What would happen if we reclaimed a day of rest? What if we blocked out space in our weeks-at-a-glance, a space where we could close down the mental and physical machinery and just be? Is it possible to put brackets around one day of the week to distinguish it as a day unlike all others, a day which truly would be the source of the new week, the wellspring of fresh energy for six more days of work?

Sunday's Dual Purpose

Early Christians began celebrating Christ's resurrection on Sunday. They consciously distinguished the day of their worship service from the Jewish Sabbath, however. Until the fourth century, when Emperor Constantine proclaimed it a public holiday, Sunday was still a regular work day. Only gradually was the Sabbath day of rest idea added to the Christian commemoration of the resurrection. Not until the sixth century did it become a requirement that Christians abstain from all work on Sunday. But tension remains to this day as to whether Sunday is primarily a day of rest or a day for meeting together to encourage each other in the work of the church.

For most of us, Sunday has come to have a dual purpose, one originating from the Jewish rest-day tradition and one from the traditional service of remembrance in honor of Christ's resurrection. Understanding the origin of each purpose can help us to be more deliberate about making space for *both* intentions—rest and corporate worship.

Holy Moments at Home in the Everyday

The home is a natural setting for short worship services, like the Sabbath meal or the Eucharist. Private homes were the first places of Christian worship. Families and friends gathered together in each others' homes to pray and share a meal together, as it says in Acts 2:46: "They broke bread in their homes and ate together with glad and sincere hearts, praising God...."

The "Lord's Supper" brought a holy moment into the heart of everyday life. Christ used, not abstract concepts, but bread and wine from the supper table to testify to his supreme redemptive work. By their very everydayness, the bread and wine became powerful symbols of the incarnation. The miracle is that as we break ordinary bread, our eyes are opened to the extraordinary. By eating and drinking "in remembrance of me" we are brought into the presence of the Redeemer and are given strength for the journey.

"We know Him in the breaking of bread," writes Dorothy Day, "and we know each other in the breaking of bread, and we are not alone any more. Heaven is a banquet and life is a banquet, too, even with a crust, where there is companionship." And that companionship is perhaps most naturally found in the intimacy and warmth of our homes.

Listening To Silence

A weekly period of intense prayer will make it easier to carry a prayerful sensitivity into our daily routines. Contemplative silence may be one fruit of a day of rest or may need to find its own time and place.

Choosing to take a short retreat in one's own home can provide vigor throughout the rest of the week. To enhance the likelihood that members of my family will learn to "retreat," I plan to craft a "place of prayer" in our home in a single room or a secluded corner. My hope is that family members can go there to do nothing but be still before God and while there, they will be interrupted respectfully and only in great need. By practicing and respecting periods of silence, we teach our children to listen to the language of silence.

Listening expectantly with our children for the natural sounds of silence teaches them to develop an ear for the still, small voice of the Spirit: tuning into faint forest sounds, quietly sitting on a rock, waiting expectantly for a twig to crack, a bird to sing, the wind to whine or flutter through the trees.

And while sitting quietly to listen with a child, we may also *see* things that we usually walk right by. One evening as I sat with our two sons watching and listening to a storm blow in, Joseph's eyes followed an ant's exploration. "I wish I could get as small as an ant," he said. "Then I could go down in those cracks in the sidewalk. I could ride on a bird. I could climb way up in a tree and rock

45

with the wind." Mystery. Wonder. Celebration!

Silence is our guide into mystery—into the boundless joy of communion with God. There is joy in sound, yes, and great joy in its absence. There are heartfelt prayers of words, yes, and a prayer for which we can find no words.

Home-Based Weekly Rituals

The weekly rituals I have selected fall into several categories: home worship services, family meal, play and work suggestions and a family covenant. These are not meant to be exhaustive but to spark ideas that any individual, family or small group could develop in its own way.

31. One Family's Saturday Work Day

Every Saturday morning at the Shuford home is family work-morning. Bob and Lois have organized their work day so that each child is responsible for age-appropriate jobs and derives satisfaction from participating in the common work-rhythm of the family. Housecleaning is divided into four jobs, one for each child. Each job expectation is described on a note card. The cards are all put on the kitchen table in the morning. Whoever gets up and starts work first has first pick of the jobs.

All the equipment needed for each job is arranged in buckets ahead of time so there is a minimum of confusion about where to find necessary cleaning supplies. After completing the job described on the card, the child signs and dates the card. Having made a contribution to the common family work, each child then cleans his or her own room. Mom and Dad do supervisory and maintenance jobs.

Throughout the morning, music fills the air. Everyone takes a break together in the middle of the morning for a snack.

At times, the Shufords have divided the jobs on a rotating basis so that each child regularly receives a turn at each job.

32. Sabbath Meal Celebration

Several families at Reba Place regularly celebrate a modified "Sabbath meal" in their homes on Saturday evening, in preparation for the coming day of worship and rest. As a delightful family worship experience, it gives a festive finish to one week while opening onto the first fine day of the new week. Like the ebb and flow of the tides, the Sabbath meal marks the ebb and flow of the week within the family setting.

The symbols of bread and wine used in the Eucharist are those used during the Sabbath meal, though with different meanings. During the Sabbath meal, when one passes the bread and wine, one is thanking God for the fruit of the earth and the fruit of the vine, an appropriate level on which to encourage children's participation. And then, as a child's knowledge of the deeper significance of the familiar symbols grows to the point where the child wants to make a commitment to Christ and to the fellowship of the church, participation in the eucharist becomes appropriate.

Bob Shuford took the Jewish Sabbath material, added a few Christian aspects, and created a responsive format especially appropriate for families with small children. An adaptation of his version is shown below.

The Shuford custom is to make the Saturday evening meal a formal dinner with linen and fine tableware. Dress for this meal is usually a touch more formal than usual. Dinner, brought on after the Sabbath ceremony, is the "big" meal of the week, making it possible to keep the Sunday meal simple, as seems appropriate for a day of rest.

Required for the ceremony itself are two candles in the center of the table, a glass of wine or grape juice and a piece of bread on a small plate.

When the children are small, the responsive format of the reading below is most appropriate. As the children grow older, all can join in reading portions of the celebration. During the Advent season, the Shufords replace the Sabbath celebration with Advent activities.

I. Candle Lighting

(*All are seated, room is dark. Parent or oldest child is ready to light the candles. Younger children cover their eyes.*)

Leader (parent, single adult or child): God said...

All: Let there be light...

(As candles are lighted, children uncover their eyes.)

Leader: Blessed are you, O Lord our God, who has hallowed us by your living word and taught us to kindle the Sabbath light.

II. Welcoming and Explaining the Sabbath

Leader: God commanded: "Six days shall you labor and do all your work, but the seventh day is the Sabbath, set aside for the Lord your God." On that day...

All: We rest.

Leader: We rest from our work, putting aside workday thoughts and cares, and celebrating the gift of life and love in our family and in the family of God. On that day...

All: We remember.

Leader: We remember that God made the whole world. God cares for us as a father and mother care for their own children. We remember that God sent Jesus, God's only son, as teacher, healer and redeemer for all the world. And we remember how God has cared for us this week. So tonight...

All: We get ready.

Leader: Tonight we get ready for tomorrow's worship, to receive our Lord, as a bride is made ready to receive the bridegroom. Let God's spirit of love come now and bind us together in harmony and peace. Together...

All: Let us welcome the day of the Lord!

III. Blessing the children

Father or Mother: On this day we thank you, God, for _____, (each child in turn). May the Lord bless you and take care of you; may the Lord be kind and gracious to you; may the Lord look on you with favor and give you peace.

(As they say this, father or mother may move around table and place hands on children's heads as the blessing is given.)

IV. Blessing the Wine and Bread

Leader: *(Fills glass and holds it up.)*

Blessed are you, O Lord our God, who has provided us with the fruit of the vine. *(Others' glasses are filled, and all drink together.)*

(Continued)

Leader: (*Holds up bread.*)
Blessed are you, O Lord our God, who has provided us with bread. (*Bread is broken and passed around the table, and all eat together.*)

Leader: The Sabbath has begun. Let us celebrate God's care for us and for the whole world.

(Family prayers; family song.)

The meal is brought on following the celebration. Conversation may focus on thanksgiving for the Lord's care in the past week.

33. Alternative Sabbath Celebration

Sara Ewing, who grew up in a Jewish home, outlined a more authentically Jewish Sabbath service which her young family uses. The order of the service below and the elements included are fairly consistent with what is done in a Jewish home on Friday evening. The Ewings celebrate the beginning of the Sabbath on Saturday evening, however, because as Jewish Christians, Sara explained, "Sunday is our day for worship and rest." Like the Shufords, the Ewings also dress up their Sabbath table and participate in family activities following the meal.

Sunday at the Ewing home is deliberately restful with a lot of reading and very little picking up of toys.

*Shabbat**

Light Candles: (*Mother usually lights the two candles in the center of the table.*)

Bless Children: (*Father places his hands on each child in turn and prays the traditional prayer, adding, as he chooses, any words specific to each child.*)

The Lord bless you and keep you;
the Lord make his face shine upon you
and be gracious to you;
the Lord turn his face toward you

and give you peace.

Remember the Sabbath Day: *(Read by Father.)*

Remember the Sabbath day by keeping it holy.
Six days you shall labour, and do all your work,
but the seventh day is a Sabbath
to the Lord your God.
On it you shall not do any work,
neither you, nor your son or daughter,
your manservant or maidservant,
nor your animals,
nor the alien within your gates.
For in six days the Lord made the heavens
and the earth, the sea and all that is in them.
But he rested on the seventh day.
Therefore, the Lord blessed the sabbath day
and made it holy.

Read one traditional Sabbath Psalm: Psalm 29, 92, 93, 95, 96, 97, 98, or 99.

Shema: *(Read together.)*

Hear, O Israel: the Lord our God, the Lord is One.
Love the Lord your God with all your heart
and with all your soul
and with all your strength.
These commandments that I give you today
are to be upon your hearts.
Talk about them when you sit at home
and when you walk along the road,
when you lie down and when you get up.
Tie them as symbols on your hands
and bind them on your foreheads.
Write them on the door frames of your houses
and on your gates.

Kiddush: *(Holding up cup, Father reads.)*

You are blessed, Lord our God,
King of the universe,
you who created the fruit of the vine.
(All drink.)

Ha-Motzi: *(Holding up bread, Father reads.)*

You are blessed, Lord our God,

King of the universe,
you who have brought bread forth from the earth.
   (*All eat.*)
(*The sharing of a meal then follows.*)

*See note on page 32 about use of inclusive language.

34. A Weekday Liturgy for the Eucharist

The Eucharist, though rarely shared within one exclusive family setting, is shared occasionally or on a weekly basis within small-group gatherings in Reba Place homes. In a small chapel in the basement of a home, it is offered every day for those who feel a special need of encouragement. The liturgy shown below is an example of liturgies that have been meaningful in such celebrations. It is adapted from a liturgical book entitled *Bread Blessed and Broken* that various people at Reba Place have found useful in planning small-group worship.

*Light**

Leader:
Father, we praise you and bless you because you do not hide from us, but reveal yourself in creation.

Group:
Your works proclaim love and concern for us. We thank you for these gifts.

Leader:
For being a Father of Light and sharing your brilliance with us, we give you thanks.

Group:
You created us in your image, you made us to walk in light. But we sinned. Confused and often lost, we preferred to walk in darkness.

Leader:
We thank you, Father, that we cannot hide from you, that you

seek us out and find us even in our darkness.

Group:

So we join all of creation, that basks in your love, in proclaiming your glory as we say: Holy, holy, holy Lord.

Leader:

We thank you, Father, for appointing your Son as a covenant to the people, a Light for all nations. He has come to open the eyes of the blind, to free captives from prison and to bring into the Light all who dwell in darkness.

Group:

Your light, Jesus Christ, has penetrated our darkness and shown us the way from selfishness to love, from isolation to community, from death to life. We thank you, Father, that Jesus is our Light and has called us to be lights to the world. We thank you for his life and example.

Leader:

But most of all, we thank you, Father, for the wonderful way Jesus strengthens us to be lights for the world.

Group:

On the night before he died, Jesus gathered his friends together. He reminded them where they came from and what they were to be. He strengthened them for their mission through a meal.

Leader:

While they were at supper he took some bread, blessed you, Father, and gave it to them saying: Take this and eat, all of you. This is my body given up to you. (*Pass the bread and eat.*)

Then he took the cup filled with wine. Again he thanked you, Father, and gave it to them saying: Take this and drink, all of you. This is the cup of my blood poured out for you and all people so sins may be forgiven. Do this in memory of me. (*Pass the cup and drink.*)

Group:

Gratefully, we remember Jesus' life among us, a life of light and love. We remember in Jesus' suffering and death the cost of being a light for one another. And finally, we constantly call to mind the hope of a new and fuller life where darkness is dispelled forever.

Leader:

And so together we proclaim our paschal faith:

All: Christ has died,

(Continued)

Christ is risen,
Christ will come again.

Leader:

Send us, Father, the Spirit Jesus promised us: the Spirit that
gives direction to our weary feet and light to our pilgrim path.
Help us discover the places where you dwell. Open our eyes to
your presence in us, our brothers, our sisters and our world.

Group:

Finally, we pray that through this meal we may be strengthened
in our resolve to become more what you want us to be: your
community of love and lights to the world.

Leader:

All of this we ask through Christ, our Light.

All:

Through him,
with him,
in him,
in the unity of the Holy Spirit,
all glory and honor is yours,
almighty Father,
forever and ever.
Amen.

*See note on page 32 about use of inclusive language.

35. Family Night Ideas

At the Shuford home, a Family Night follows the Sabbath meal,
an evening reserved for doing fun activities together as a family in
the spirit of the Sabbath. Several times a year the Shufords draw
up a list of suggested activities with everyone contributing ideas.
They then choose activities from this list as specific Family Nights
approach. Some family nights have included playing children's
trivia games, charades, going out for ice cream, watching selected
videos, ice-skating, singing together, and a variety of other
activities.

36. Once-A-Week-Dinner-Special

At the Vogt home when the children were younger, there was a once-a-week-dinner-special. Each of the children took turns choosing the menu for that particular evening. Each could choose whatever he or she wanted and had a lot of fun doing it. Lots of homemade french fries and onion rings turned up in those days. The once-a-week-super-duper menu helped balance out the fact that on other days of the week, the Vogts were operating resourcefully on a very limited budget.

Other weekly food rituals in the Vogt home included waffles on Saturday mornings, and a fresh batch of chocolate chip cookies on Friday afternoons.

37. A Family Meeting Night

The Taylor family has a once-a-week family meeting night. Monday evening, usually during dinner, is the time for family discussions related to the week's plans, work schedules, and any problem areas in family relationships.

Cindy discovered that since she was home more than her husband, the children were coming to her with most of their concerns and many decisions were being made without input from Dad. In order to bring more balance into the decision-making process, Monday evening was set aside for just such deliberations. Now Mom will say, "Can that decision wait until Monday when we can discuss it as a family?" The family meeting night has facilitated a fairer distribution of responsibility for family decisions.

38. A Family Covenant of Children's Just Deserts

Our society is failing millions of its teenage young. Social indicators show that the well-being of adolescents has declined sharply since 1960. Evidence is everywhere, from test scores on college admissions tests to the increasing number of violent deaths. North American teenagers have the highest pregnancy rate among industrialized nations. Delinquency rates have gone up sharply since 1960, as have death rates due to accidents, homicides and suicides. Children grow up in a society where drugs are prevalent, where there are few generally agreed-on constraints on sexual activity and where violence is constantly celebrated on television. It is not easy to grow up in North America.

What can be done to strengthen families so that children will have the inner strength to counter the forces that undermine our best efforts?

I have drawn up a list of "Children's Just Deserts" which we try to infuse into our family life. Perhaps pinning such a list up on a bulletin board or refrigerator for weekly reference could be one small way of reminding ourselves about what is truly important for our children. Each family could compose its own list and revise it from time to time.

Children's Just Deserts

1. Children deserve a mother who makes sure she finds the support and nurture she needs so she can wholeheartedly love them.
2. Children deserve a father who loves their mother so much that he'll cook sometimes and fold diapers, vacuum the floor and tuck her into bed.
3. Children deserve a mother who likes herself, who has creative work that she enjoys in addition to childcare.
4. Children deserve a father who likes his work and wants his children to know about it and why it's important.
5. Children deserve a mother who gets rid of clutter, who knows how to conserve, recycle and keep things simple.
6. Children deserve a father who thanks his wife for the supper

even when it's burned, and who remembers when his son spills the milk that he used to spill the milk too.

7. Children deserve a mother or father who will rock them to sleep with a lullaby and tuck them into bed with a story and with prayer.

8. Children deserve a father who will take them for a walk through the fall leaves rather than buying them another toy.

9. Children deserve a mother or father who takes them to the library every other week and comes home with armloads of books about people who dream great dreams and overcome immense difficulties.

10. Children deserve a mother and father who are willing to slow down from the rat race long enough to enter into the wonder of disovery with them.

11. Children deserve a mother and father who will allow them to work alongside, at their own pace, and with appropriate jobs so that each can feel a sense of accomplishment on completion.

12. Children deserve a mother and father who are very selective about television watching, who study the program guide to know what quality programs exist and who will spend time reading or playing games instead of lazily flicking on the switch.

13. Children deserve a mother and father who participate in a church fellowship where young people are a central part of the worship life.

14. Children deserve a mother and father who have an extended family network of support and back-up nurture.

15. Children deserve a mother and father who know how to celebrate in honor of the Giver of all truly good gifts.

Chapter Four
Yearly Festivities

The year waxes and wanes—seedtime and harvest, springtime and winter, birth and death.

People from the Judeo-Christian heritage have traditionally celebrated a cycle of festivals which resonates with the seasonal rhythm. The church festivals, year after year, give celebrants a sense of belonging to a community of faith that stretches back through the ages.

The Church Year faded somewhat from our collective memory under the onslaught of industrialization and the prunings of Puritanism. It deserves a revival. Its reliable structure of meaning gives direction to those of us prone to wander off on tangents or to be lured into overly commercialized hoopla.

In small but regular ways, every twelve months, the decisive events of faith history are replayed. We are invited to imaginatively participate in historic events which we believe continue to affect our present. Every year as we grow older and perhaps wiser, the events wend their way through our deepening understanding, bringing new insights. Every year we join with thousands of God's people through the centuries and around the world in recounting and celebrating God's marvelous works.

As families, we are fortunate to be able to tap into the immense resources of Church Year traditions. Annual festivities provide the basic framework on which to shape celebrations that suit the needs of our own families. And then as celebrations return every year, they pick up momentum. Creativity builds on what has happened in the past.

Children come to rely on the return of a pleasant, memorable event year after year. A heritage of good childhood memories, reinforced by the rhythmic cycle of yearly celebrations, will help to carry our children safely to the end of their days.

Many of the celebrations that follow fit into the framework of the Church Year as it is observed at Reba Place. I haven't attempted to include a family-based event for every religiously significant day but rather to include those events that have come to be most meaningful for folks in this church, year after year.

Advent Traditions

The season of Advent begins with the fourth Sunday before Christmas. The word "advent" means "coming" or "arrival." Advent is the season of the Church Year in which we prepare for the coming of our Lord at Christmas. We think of this preparation in three ways:

1. The centuries of preparation for Christ's coming as seen in the Old Testament.
2. The preparation that we as individuals and as families make for the coming of Christ into our lives.
3. The looking forward to the time when Christ will be recognized by all people everywhere as King of kings and Lord of lords.

39. Advent Wreath

A delightful family-worship custom can be used to bring us to readiness for Christmas day. From early church history there has been the tradition of using the Advent Wreath and its candles to set apart the Sundays of this expectant season. First records of the wreath show it as a holly and evergreen garland, holding four small candles and one large central candle. One of the small candles was lit the first Sunday of Advent, and each succeeding Sunday another was lit, until, immediately before Christmas, all four small candles were burning brightly. On Christmas day the large center candle was lit.

In our day there seems to be no universal tradition for the color of the candles. Some use purple candles; some use red or white. One common practice at Reba Place is to have four purple candles and one large white candle in the center. Purple has traditionally been the color that reminds us of repentance—an appropriate reminder as we prepare again for Christ's coming. Purple is also the color of kings, reminding us that Jesus Christ is King.

The round wreath can be made from evergreen branches, its round shape reminding us that God had no beginning and will have no end. The circle of greenery can also signify God's unending love for us.

The wreath can be constructed in any number of imaginative ways and with a variety of materials.

1. Simply set the four purple candles and holders in a circle on the table, placing the large white candle in the middle of the circle. Surround the candles with evergreens or holly to resemble a wreath.

2. Make an Advent candleboard which can be used again each year.

    a) Cut a square of wood about one foot square and at least 1/2 inch thick.

    b) Bore 5 holes with a 5/8 inch drill bit (the same size as the candles), 1 inch in from each corner and one in the center. Make them deep enough to hold the candles firmly.

    c) Sand the board until smooth.

    d) Paint with dark green paint. If you wish, when the board is dry, letter "Come, Lord Jesus" with a contrasting color.

    e) Place standard size purple tapers in corners, white in center.

    f) Place evergreen boughs over board and display in a prominent place.

40. Advent Weekly Worship Service

A family Advent Worship Service may be held before or after supper, just before bedtime, or at some other time convenient for the entire family. Begin on the first Sunday of Advent, four Sundays before Christmas.

Everyone in the family may have a part in the service. One child may light the candles, another snuff them out. Another may read the scripture passage, offer a prayer or choose an Advent song. If Christmas carols are reserved until Christmas day and beyond, their joy will ring more true for the waiting.

If you wish, during the week read the additional suggested scriptures in sequence and light that week's candles for only a short time.

On the second, third and fourth Sundays continue the celebration, adding the second, third and fourth candle lightings, readings and verses of the Advent hymn, "O Come, O Come Emmanuel." (Perhaps the oldest child could light the first candle, the second child the second, a parent the third, etc., each reading again why he or she lights the candle.) On Christmas day, light the center candle.

The following Advent Service is adapted from several services that have been used in Reba Place homes.

The Advent Celebration

Call to Worship (used every week)
> **Leader:** The people walking in darkness have seen a great light;
> **All:** On those living in the land of the shadow of death a light has dawned.
> **Leader:** For to us a child is born, to us a son is given, and the government will be on his shoulders.
> **All:** And he will be called Wonderful Counselor, Mighty God, Everlasting Father, Prince of Peace.

First Week of Advent
> Scripture reading: Isaiah 9:7
>
> *As first candle is lit say:*
> I light this candle in memory of God's promise to send a Leader who will deliver all people from oppression and injustice.

Sing: O come, O come, Emmanuel,
   And ransom captive Israel,
   That mourns in lonely exile here,
   Until the Son of God appear.
    Refrain: Rejoice! Rejoice! Emmanuel
      Shall come to thee, O Israel!

Suggested scripture readings for first week:

Monday	Isaiah 11:1–3a	Thursday Isaiah 11:10
Tuesday	Isaiah 11:3b–5	Friday	Isaiah 12:1–3
Wednesday	Isaiah 11:6–9	Saturday	Isaiah 12:4–6

Second Week of Advent

Scripture reading: Isaiah 40:1–5, 41:13

Light the first candle, repeating what was said earlier.

Light the second candle, saying:
  I light this candle in memory
  of God's promise to send a Comforter
  and Saviour.

Sing: (Repeat first verse of "O Come, O Come Emmanuel"
  and add the second.)
  O come, Thou Dayspring, come and cheer
  Our spirits by Thine advent here;
  Disperse the gloomy clouds of night,
  And death's dark shadows put to flight.
   Refrain: Rejoice! Rejoice! Emmanuel
    Shall come to thee, O Israel!

Suggested scripture readings for second week:

Monday	Isaiah 40:10–11	Thursday Isaiah 42:14–16
Tuesday	Isaiah 42:1–4	Friday	Isaiah 51:4–6
Wednesday	Isaiah 42:5–9	Saturday	Isaiah 53:1–6

Third Week of Advent

Scripture reading: John 1:1–5, 8:12

Light the first and second candles in turn.

Light the third candle, saying:
  I light this candle for Jesus Christ
  who is the Light of the world.

Sing: (Repeat the first two verses of "O Come, O Come
  Emmanuel" and add the third.)

(Continued)

O come, Thou Key of David, come,
And open wide our heav'nly home;
Make safe the way that leads on high.
And close the path to misery.
Refrain: Rejoice! Rejoice! Emmanuel
Shall come to thee, O Israel!

Suggested scripture readings for third week:

Monday	John 1:6–8	Thursday	John 1:19–23
Tuesday	John 1:9–13	Friday	John 1:24–28
Wednesday	John 1:14–18	Saturday	John 1:29–34

Fourth Week of Advent

Scripture reading: Luke 1:26–33

Light first, second and third candles in turn.

Light the fourth candle, saying:
I light this candle for Jesus Christ
whose Kingdom will have no end.

Sing: (Repeat the first three verses of "O Come, O Come
Emmanuel" and add the fourth.)
O come, Thou Lord of nations, bind
All peoples in one heart and mind;
Bid envy, strife and quarrels cease;
Fill the whole world with heaven's peace.
Refrain: Rejoice! Rejoice! Emmanuel
Shall come to thee, O Israel!

Suggested scripture readings for fourth week, until Christmas day:

Monday	I John 4:7–9	Thursday	I John 4:13–16
Tuesday	I Peter 2:9–10	Friday	I John 5:1–5
Wednesday	Philippians 4:4–7	Saturday	I John 5:10–12

Christmas Day

Christmas scripture: Luke 2:1–20

Light first four candles in turn.

Light the Christ candle, saying:
I light this candle for Jesus Christ
who was born in a lowly manger.

Sing: O come, all ye faithful, joyful and triumphant,
O come ye, O come ye to Bethlehem;

Come and behold Him, Born the King of angels;
Refrain: O come, let us adore Him,
O come, let us adore Him,
O, come let us adore Him,
Christ the Lord.

Sing more Christmas carols as time allows.

41. An Advent Calendar

Sara Ewing made a colorful felt Advent Calendar for her family. It serves two basic purposes: 1) simply to mark off the days of Advent as Christmas approaches, 2) to emphasize our Jewish heritage by featuring Old Testament prophecies and their fulfillment in Jesus.

The felt calendar is easy to construct, durable and instructive:

a) Use a large 2- by 3-foot piece of felt of any favorite color.

b) Cut 24 small white squares of felt.

c) Glue a symbol (also cut from various colored pieces of felt) for each day of Advent onto each white square. The suggested symbols accompany each day's reading and are indicated in parentheses . Each of the 24 white squares will be a small intact piece.

d) Fasten Velcro® to the back of each of the 24 squares. Velcro® can be machine-sewn onto the large felt piece—four across and six down. Each square is affixed to the large felt backing on its appropriate day. The calendar will look something like this on December 24:

(Continued)

Advent Readings to Accompany Calendar

1. Deuteronomy 18:15–19 (Tablets)

God chose Moses to lead the people of Israel out of Egypt. They traveled for forty years. When they were near their new home, God spoke to Moses on a mountain. One of the things God told Moses was that God would send another person to speak for God after Moses died. This did not happen for many, many years. Then God sent us Jesus, the son, whose birth we celebrate at Christmas.

2. II Samuel 7:11b–16 (Crown)

For a time the people of Israel had kings to rule them. David was one of the kings. God said that the new person who would speak for God would be an ancestor of David. That is why we will read later that Jesus is born of the house and lineage of David.

3. Psalm 89:19–37 (Heart)

God would choose to honor one of King David's descendants. He would be called the one God chose, the firstborn, the highest of the kings of the earth. God would establish a wonderful kingdom with Jesus as the King because of God's great love for all people.

4. Isaiah 11:1–9 (Shoot from Stump)

Isaiah the prophet said that a descendant would arise from Jesse, David's father, and the spirit of the Lord would rest upon him. Jesus came as that righteous man who did all things through the guidance of God's spirit. Jesus will come again to bring the kingdom of peace where the wolf and the lamb can lie down together.

5. Isaiah 7:13–14 (word: IMMANUEL)

God said that the Messiah would be born of a virgin and would be called Immanuel, meaning God-with-us.

6. Micah 5:2–4 (Building and Palms)

God said that the Messiah would be born in Bethlehem.

7. Daniel 2:36–45 (Image and Stone)

King Nebuchadnezzar had a dream that Daniel interpreted. In the dream there was a great image which was broken by a great stone. The image represented all the kingdoms of the earth and the stone represented God's Kingdom with Jesus as Lord.

8. Jeremiah 33:14–16 (Tree and Branch)

Jeremiah reassured a hopeless people that God would really bring the Messiah, the righteous branch to spring forth from the line of David.

9. Isaiah 61:1–3 (Chain, broken)

Isaiah told of some of the things that the Messiah would do—comfort the sad, free the prisoners, preach good news to the poor, bring us gladness and help us to walk with God.

10. Isaiah 53 (Cross)

God said that the Messiah would come to suffer and die for our sins and take away our sicknesses.

11. Isaiah 40:1–2 (word: COMFORT)

The people of Israel thought it was taking a long time for God to send the Messiah. They asked, "How long, O Lord, how long?" God sent comfort to them and said to wait and see. God would really bring it to pass.

12. Isaiah 40:3–4 (Crooked Line, Mountain)

God sent someone to prepare the way for Jesus. John, Jesus' cousin, was that man. He called people to repentance.

13. Luke 1:5–23 (Temple)

Zechariah was a priest married to Elizabeth. They wanted a child but they were too old. When Zechariah was in the temple in Jerusalem, the angel Gabriel appeared to him and said that he and Elizabeth would have a son. Zechariah didn't believe the message God sent through the angel, so the angel told Zechariah that he would be unable to talk until his son was born.

14. Luke 1:26–38 (Angel and Mary, kneeling)

Gabriel was sent by God to Nazareth to Mary, a virgin engaged to a man named Joseph. The angel told Mary that she would bear a son who would be called Jesus. Jesus would be the promised descendant of David who would reign forever. He would be the Messiah.

15. Luke 1:39–56 (Two Women, holding hands)

Mary went to visit her cousin Elizabeth, who was pregnant with John, the son God had promised them. Both Mary and Elizabeth were going to have special children sent by God. Elizabeth's son was to prepare the way for Mary's son who would be Jesus, the Messiah.

16. Luke 1:57–66 (Hebrew letters spelling: JOHN) יוֹחָנָן

Finally Elizabeth's baby was born. Zechariah wrote that the baby's name was to be John. Immediately Zechariah was able to talk again.

(Continued)

17. Matthew 1:18–25 (Hebrew letters spelling: JESUS) יֵשׁוּעַ

Joseph had a hard time believing God had given Mary a special son, so God sent the angel Gabriel to Joseph to reassure him that what Mary said was true. The angel said to name the child, Jesus, which means saviour.

18. Luke 2:1–3 (Coins)

In the city of Rome, Emperor Augustus sent a message out to all the people. A messenger brought the message to Nazareth where Joseph and Mary lived. He said, "The Emperor cannot rule such a huge empire without lots of money! Therefore, in order that taxes may be properly collected, the Emperor orders all men, with their wives, to return to the town where they were born. There they must be counted and listed."

19. Luke 2:4–5 (Donkey)

Joseph and Mary went to Bethlehem, their birth place. They knew it would be a difficult trip since Mary was expecting the baby so soon.

20. Luke 2:6–7 (Stable)

Joseph and Mary looked and looked for a place to stay but all the inns were full. So they stayed in a stable with the animals and slept on the hay.

21. Matthew 2:1–12 (Star)

A special star appeared in the sky at Jesus' birth. Three wise men came to worship Jesus because of the star they saw.

22. Luke 2:8–12 (Shepherds)

The angel appeared to the shepherds outside of Bethlehem and told them of Jesus' birth.

23. Luke 2:13–15 (Angels)

Many angels appeared to the shepherds, giving glory to God.

24. Luke 2:16–20 (Manger)

The shepherds came to the place where Jesus lay, a tiny baby wrapped in cloth lying in a manger (a place where animals eat). Jesus was a special baby and would grow up to make it possible for all of us to become God's people.

42. Preparing a Place for Jesus' Coming

The Shuford family has an interesting custom that adds meaning to the traditional creche. They explain, "During Advent we gradually build up the straw in Jesus' manger by doing good turns for each other. For each deed you can place another straw in the manger. The idea is to prepare a place for Jesus' coming on Christmas day. In the past, you could make anyone in the family the object of your good will; this year we will experiment with assignments, being some *one's* secret angel.

"The creche is empty except for the accumulating straw. Mary and Joseph make their long trek across the living room, from one spot to another, until they arrive Christmas Eve at the creche next to the dining room table. The animals, shepherds and angels also join the scene, having gathered one at a time, all during Advent."

43. "Decking the Halls," Week by Week

Brigitte Krummel suggests that rather than bringing all the festive decorations out at once, the pleasure of getting ready for Christmas is enhanced if each Advent Sunday something new is brought out. For example, on the second Sunday of Advent, Brigitte brings out the wooden frame for the candy and gingerbread house which is reconstructed by the children and invited friends with new sweets each year. On the third Sunday of Advent, she brings out the empty manger. The various figurines are dispersed throughout the house. The children move them closer and closer to the manger with several new arrivals each day. The three kings come from far away. Mary and Joseph are very late in coming. Jesus doesn't arrive until Christmas Eve.

44. Selecting a Family Creche

Neta Jackson notes that a primary consideration when her family selected a creche was finding a manger and figurines that could be touched and played with. The Jacksons chose a wooden creche. And in their home, as in other Reba Place homes, the children progressively move the shepherds, wise men, Mary, Joseph and Jesus toward the manger.

45. Singing Carols Around the Creche

Judy Belser related a cozy Advent custom that her family enjoys which is especially appropriate for families with small children. Many evenings during Advent they turn out all the lights except the Christmas lights and candles. Then while sitting around the creche, they simply sing carols like "Away in a Manger" and "The Friendly Beasts" until bedtime.

Judy also described how placing a small gift at the plate of each child for the Advent candle lighting service adds to the small children's anticipation and joy during the celebration.

46. Advent Scripture-Mirror-Candle Ritual

Michelle Lazar has developed a simple ritual in her home to enhance the spirit of Advent. She places a candle in front of her bathroom mirror, a much frequented spot in the house. Each day Michelle sets a card behind the candle on which is written a scriptural promise or admonition. When she puts a new card behind the candle each day, Michelle tapes the old card higher up on another part of the mirror. By the end of the Advent season the mirror is nearly filled with memorable and thought-provoking scriptures.

47. Cookies at Advent

Joan Vogt remarks that when her children were young Advent was a time to make cookies—lots of cookies and all kinds of cookies. But none were to be eaten before Christmas Eve. All the cookies were stored in large glass jars, and only on Christmas Eve would they be available for the cookie trays.

48. Telling Family History with Tree Ornaments

Neta Jackson says that each year her family buys a new Christmas tree ornament that commemorates a significant family event from that particular year. The ornament may depict something noteworthy about a special family trip, a baby's arrival, a new pet, or a new job for Dad. The Jacksons have accumulated some 20 such ornaments, which in their own way retell the family history over a 20-year span every time they are lovingly placed on the tree. The older ornaments show a lot of wear but are especially cherished.

49. Lanterns for Christmas Caroling

Hilda Carper describes a simple, beautiful lantern for Christmas carollers: a candle set in a jar serves both as a hand warmer and as a welcome light. The jars can be decorated on the outside with colorful tissue paper cut in attractive patterns.

Christmas Eve Festivities

Christmas traditions vary among families at Reba Place. Some will have a family worship service on Christmas Eve, accompanied by gift-giving. Others will wait until Christmas day for the climax of the season. Many of the families attend a church Christmas Eve service early in the evening before retiring to their homes for family celebrations. Midnight Mass is a powerful festival in the Catholic Christian tradition which individual families may want to make a regular feature of their family Christmas Eve tradition.

50. A Candle-Lighting Ceremony

The Ewing family goes to an early Christmas Eve service. After returning home, they have Christmas cookies, hot chocolate and cider together.

A candle-lighting ceremony follows the goodies. A tray filled with unlit candles is placed on the table. Each person in the family takes turns lighting a candle from the Christ candle, one at a time, mentioning someone's name with each candle and saying a short prayer for that person—that he or she will be brought to the light of Christ. The children help to name individuals and, as they are able, help with the candle lighting and prayers. After all the candles are lit, the family sings Christmas carols together until bedtime.

51. Birthday Cake for Jesus

The Shufords hold a birthday celebration on Christmas Eve: "When we arrive home from the early Christmas Eve service, we'll have a birthday cake and sing the traditional 'Happy Birthday to You' to Jesus. At this point baby Jesus (kept hidden until now) is placed in the stable. As the children grow older the focus shifts from the babe in the manger to a birthday celebration for a resurrected Lord."

52. A "Complete" Evening

In the Krummel home, Christmas Eve is the climax of the season. Brigitte cooks in the morning for the evening meal so that she will need only to warm the food at mealtime. Then as the evening approaches, busyness recedes and peace settles over the household. Brigitte turns on music and takes a bath. At 4 or 5 o'clock the family shares tea, coffee and Christmas cookies (the first they've been eaten). Then after church, they enjoy the evening meal.

Following the meal, all move to the creche for a worship service. The big Christ candle is lit for the first time. Each person, children included, comes prepared to contribute a poem, a scripture or a song. Following the readings and songs each person selects a candle from a tray of candles and lights it for himself or herself, placing it somewhere around the creche. A supply of extra candles is available if anyone wants to light several for others, naming each person as the candle is lit from the Christ candle and perhaps saying a sentence prayer for that person. All the candles are placed one by one around the creche.

After a hearty wish all around for a Merry Christmas, the gifts are distributed and opened one by one. A new family game under the tree every year brings the family members together to play during the evening. Doing something together as a family has been very significant for the children. When the festivities die down, the last one to bed blows out the Christ candle. The first one up in the morning lights it again.

Christmas Day Traditions

53. Simple Fun and Relaxation

Christmas day at the Krummel home, after the festivities of the evening before (see above), is a day for fun and relaxation. The Christmas turkey, prepared in advance, needs only to be popped into the oven. The turkey, accompanied by a sizeable salad, provides the delectable basics for the Christmas dinner. The turkey stays on the table the rest of the afternoon so that folks can help themselves whenever they feel inclined to nibble.

54. Candle-Lighting, Gift for Jesus, and Gift Exchange

The Shufords describe their family Christmas morning routine:

"Begin with the house dark. Light the Jesus candle, at the center of the dining room table. Each one has at his/her place a candle, which is lighted from the Jesus candle with the good news, 'The light of Christ has come into the world.' Then with our own candles lit, we light the many candles which have been placed around the living and dining rooms. Sing together, 'Joy to the World,' and put on a Christmas record. It's a beautiful scene to begin Christmas day.

"Next, we all give our gifts to Jesus (something symbolic that each of us has prepared as his or her own heartfelt love gift). When the kids were toddlers, they would 'give' a special toy (like a small matchbox car); as they got a little older, we were able to help them make something (Gabe and Bob made a small bed about 3 inches long for Jesus). This year we may try written pledges, as we parents have done all along. At any rate, we do this right after the candles, before starting into our own gifts.

"Gifts are exchanged one-by-one. Becky, as the oldest child, selects each gift from under the tree and hands it to the *giver*, who personally delivers it. Following each opening, hugs are exchanged. I think the kids appreciate the process because each gift means so much more."

55. A Family Tradition of Handmade Gifts

The Vogt family has a tradition of making handmade gifts for each other: "Early on we started making gifts for one another. This was partly a matter of necessity, since we operated on a meager budget. But it was also a matter of choice, an exciting opportunity for creative abilities. With seven in the family, this means one has to begin early. So expectations and excitement for Christmas began to build....Sometimes you could gather from choice little hints, deliberately dropped to kindle interest, that the Christmas preparations had begun already in September or October. By November and December, of course, there was a lot going on. So much love and joy went into these preparations. And keeping things secret added to the suspense and excitement."

The Vogts also suggest the idea of each member of the family giving one gift to a needy person at Christmas time, thus expanding the circle of shared love.

56. Remembering Those in Need

Sara Ewing explains that she and husband, James, have tried to minimize gift-giving in their family. In order to enhance the spirit of giving rather than getting, they have packaged mittens, woolen scarves, or special lunches to share with so-called "street people." Last Christmas they offered to go to the local shelter for the homeless to help serve Christmas breakfast.

The Ewings also make a point of inviting others who may be lonely or without their own family, to join them for Christmas or other holiday dinners.

57. Writing Stories for Gifts

Steve Holler writes children's stories for gifts at Christmas time, and sometimes for a birthday or a wedding gift.

58. A Festive Brunch and Family Talent Show

At the Jackson home on Christmas morning, a festive brunch is the tradition. It is at this brunch when the Christ candle is first lit.

Neta mentions a tradition from their extended family gathering, for each family to come prepared to contribute something in a modified talent show—a song, a funny poem, a skit or an instrumental piece. The event is an excellent way to bring adults and children together for a good, wholesome time enjoyed by all ages.

59. Making Holiday Meal Preparation a Family Affair

Carol Steiner notes that the cook often feels left out of family activities at holiday times because he or she (usually she) is too busy in the kitchen. Carol discovered that she didn't look forward to holidays because of this enormous responsibility. To avoid the burden, Carol suggests making holiday cooking a family project. Now in her family, different members sign up ahead of time for specific holiday meal tasks and food contributions. Everyone then has the satisfaction of having made the holiday a pleasant event, not only at the table, but also while working together in the kitchen.

The Steiners have a large meal on Christmas Eve and a festive brunch on Christmas morning.

Three Kings' Day

January 6 is traditionally the last of the twelve days of Christmas. It is called Epiphany or Three Kings' Day and serves to conclude the festive Christmas season.

Matthew 2:1–12 gives the scriptural orientation for the day. Matthew doesn't speak of the visitors as kings but as wise and learned men who studied the stars and diligently sought after the newborn king. These wise men serve as representatives of persons from all nations who will come to recognize Christ Jesus as Saviour and Lord.

The story of the arrival of the wise men, their joy on finding the Christ child, their worship of costly gifts is a story that takes on added poignancy if it is separated out from the rest of the Christmas events and allowed to stand on its own.

60. A Day for Small Group Gatherings and Gift Exchanges

Traditionally, Three Kings' Day at Reba Place has been the day for church small-group gatherings and gift exchanges. There may be a party, a potluck meal, charades, a reading of the wise men story and Christmas carols.

Often, members of the groups have exchanged names and then made or purchased a simple gift for the person whose name was drawn.

61. Three Wise Men Arrive at Creche

In the Shuford home the three wise men don't arrive at the creche until Epiphany. The Christmas tree and other decorations are not dismantled until this, the last day of Christmas.

New Year's Events

This is the time for the family historian, archivist and photographer to shine, a time to traverse back over the preceding year and gather together the foolish, sublime and momentous events for a night of remembering.

62. Recalling Last Year's Highlights in a Variety of Ways

There are different ways one may choose to recall and relive events from the past year. Hilda Carper suggests several possibilities:

1. Keep a brief record of memorable events throughout the year on a calendar with large date blocks, making it relatively easy to pull together an overview of the year.

2. Show slides from the past years, including groups of slides from each preceding year, for a fascinating record of change over the years.

3. Compile a family scrapbook at the end of each year. Throughout the year the family archivists collect drawings, love notes, cards, reports cards, newspaper clippings—whatever will help to tell the family story. Have a new, empty scrapbook ready for New Year's Eve. Bring out all the collected treasures. Everyone works together to fill the pages for a new Family Yearbook.

4. Celebrate with a "Blessing Cake." Using birthday candles, have each family member take a candle, mention something he or she is thankful for from the past year, light the candle and put it in the cake.

5. After putting the youngest children to bed, the older family members may want to gather at 11:00 p.m. for a watchnight service. Other friends could be invited for a time of prayer, singing and sharing in the Eucharist as the new year begins.

63. New Year's Breakfast

The Shuford family traditionally greets the New Year with a touch of class. Dad prepares a delectable, sumptuous breakfast, leaving the whole family with heightened expectations for even better things to come the rest of the year. Every New Year's morning Dad makes Eggs Benedict, with homemade (real butter) hollandaise sauce, and served with Canadian bacon or sliced ham, and with Holland Rusk or zwieback.

Valentine's Day Activities

Valentine's Day is traditionally a day to celebrate love and love's blessing of friendship. Authorities have different opinions about the holiday's origins. Some trace it to an ancient Roman fertility festival. Others connect the event to two saints named Valentine in the early Christian church. Still other experts link it with an old English belief that birds choose their mates on February 14. Actually, Valentine's Day probably comes from a combination of all three sources. And then there is the simple notion that the advent of spring is a time for love.

64. A Secret Valentine Pal

Neta Jackson says that she decorates the house for Valentine's Day. She makes a special dinner with a heart cake. The family members draw names for a secret valentine pal. During the day the secret pal may slip a bottle of pop into the refrigerator with the intended receiver's name on it. He or she may make a bed for the pal or devise any number of delightful surprises throughout the day.

65. Valentine Mobile, Cards, and Poem

The eve before Valentine's Day, after the children are in bed, Lois Shuford turns the chandelier above the dining table into a mobile of red valentines. To make the mobile, Lois cuts out a red construction paper heart for each child and writes on each, "Jesus loves (name)." She also includes a different "love" scripture reference on each heart. Each child is expected to track down his or her scripture during the day and read it aloud at dinner. A large heart in the middle of the mobile reads, "Jesus loves everyone."

In the morning the children will also find a gift wrapped in red at each of their cereal bowls.

Bob makes a valentine card for each child and writes a simple, pertinent poem especially suited for the individual child. All cards from all family members go into a box with a slit from which they are distributed at dinner.

66. A Poem for Each Year

Sara Ewing writes a poem or limerick every Valentine's Day for each of her children. The yearly rhymes have become a tradition— a treasury of poems that stretch back through years of Valentine Days.

67. Exchanging Personal Valentines

Joanna Lehman planned a small Valentine's Day party with games and treats when her children were small. Ahead of time, the family drew names to choose one person for whom to make one very special valentine. Then at the party, one by one, they shared their valentines, with the person who had just received a valentine being the next one to give his or her valentine, and so on.

68. Making Valentine Cards Instead of Christmas Cards

Instead of sending Christmas cards (which most people send and receive en masse) Peggy Belser makes and sends valentine cards to loved ones every year. And she has a lot of fun doing it away from the normal congestion of the Christmas season.

St. Patrick's Day

On March 17, we usually do little more than wear green, hang up a green shamrock or two and perhaps make a green colored cake. Yet there is a much richer meaning than "green" to this day.

While a parent may want to do research on St. Patrick to fill in the picture of this man's significance to our faith history, the play included below, written and used at Reba Place Church, could be used in a family setting with family members reading the various parts. The play's "archaic" language underlines the story's ancient setting, and, consequently, makes it most appropriate for older children and adults. Have everyone look over their parts ahead of time, doubling up on the characters if necessary, or have one person read the entire play as a dramatic story.

69. St. Patrick: Missionary to the Irish

c.389–c.461

Characters:	Patrick	Narrator
	3 Monks	Laoghaire, King of Tara
	Lucatmael, a Druid	Captain
	2nd Druid	2 Guards
	Dubtach, a Bard	Fiacc, a Bard

Scene I: The Hill of Slane. *Patrick and three monks on stage.*

Narrator: Our play begins about three years after the death of St.

Augustine. It is the middle of the night of Holy Saturday, March 25, 433 A.D., in Ireland. There have been few darker times in the history of the West or of the Christian Church than the Fifth Century. Twenty-five years before the start of today's play the Vandals crossed the Rhine and wrought devastation across Europe. A traveller at that time reports journeying across Europe for 28 days and not meeting a single living human being. In 410 A.D. the Vandals sacked Rome. In 476 A.D. the last emperor of the old Roman Empire in the West was deposed by a German chieftain. The Church, which had in the preceding four centuries spread throughout all of the known world, was also on the defensive. The Church had become corrupt and wracked with heresy. Some Christian church buildings had been converted into pagan temples.

In Ireland, a young church was struggling against the power of the Druids, the priests of the ancient religion of Gaul and Britain, whose followers practiced divination through human sacrifice. These Druids were the counselors of petty kings and were using both influence and force to prevent their subjects from accepting Christianity.

The thick darkness covering the earth can be felt by Bishop Patrick and his small band of monks who huddle together preparing to light the Paschal bonfire. The setting is the top of Slane Hill, where Patrick has recently arrived with a commission from Pope Celestine to bring Christianity to the Irish.

Patrick: Dear Friends in Christ: On this most holy night, in which our Lord Jesus Christ passed over from death to life, we keep watch together, and by hearing his Word and celebrating his Sacraments we share in his victory over death. Let us pray: O God, you have bestowed on your people the brightness of your light. Sanctify this new fire and us who light it as a sign of the resurrection of your Son, Jesus Christ.

All: Amen.

Patrick: (*lighting fire*) The Light of Christ!

Monks: Thanks be to God!

Patrick: Rejoice now, heavenly hosts and choirs of angels,
      and let your trumpets shout Salvation
      for the victory of our mighty King.

Monks: Rejoice and sing now, all the round earth,
    bright with a glorious splendor,
    for darkness has been vanquished by our eternal King.
    Rejoice and be glad now, Mother Church,
    and let your holy courts, in radiant light,
    resound with the praises of your people.

Patrick: This is the night when you brought our fathers and mothers, the children of Israel, out of bondage in Egypt and led them through the Red Sea on dry land.

Monks: This is the night when Christ broke the bonds of death and hell and rose victorious over the grave.

Patrick: Holy God, accept our evening sacrifice, the offering of this fire in your honor. May it shine continually to drive away all darkness. May Christ, the Morning Star, who knows no setting, find it ever burning—he who gives his light to all creation and who lives and reigns for ever and ever.

All: Amen. *(Pause.)*

Monk 1: It is good to see the fire blaze out. The darkness here is uncanny. It feels as if there is not a light in all of Ireland tonight. The whole country seems shrouded in darkness.

Patrick: This is true in more ways than one. I have great respect for these people. Their learning is in many ways superior to ours in Gaul and Britain. They have many books written in their language, and they know much about the stars and how to cure diseases. Their laws are written down, as are many of their stories. But their souls are lost in sin and darkness. Most of them still worship the trees and practice magic. Their lives are violent and quarrelsome. But the Lord has chosen us to bring the light of Christ to illumine their souls and enlighten their minds.

Monk 2: How do you know this land so well? We have only been here a week.

Patrick: I have been here before. I was raised in Britain by a Christian family. But when I was still young, I was kidnapped by Irish raiders and brought here as a slave. I spent six long, lonely, cold and hungry years on these barren hillsides tending my master's herds. But one night I had a dream telling me to escape, for a boat was waiting. I did, and it was.

Monk 3: Why ever did you decide to come back?

Patrick: Well, there was another dream. One night about ten years later, a man named Victorious appeared to me in a dream and handed me a letter. It was from someone called "Voice of the Irish." It begged me to "come back and walk again among us." I must confess, it did not come upon me naturally to want to help those who had taken me captive. But who am I to argue with God? I travelled to Gaul and began my studies for the ministry. And in his time the Lord gave me this mission.
(*Lucatmael and 2nd Druid burst in.*)

Lucatmael: Put out that fire, by order of the King of Tara!

Patrick: No. It must burn on.

Lucatmael: Who are you, Stranger? Why have you lit a fire in defiance of the High King of Ireland? Don't you know that anyone who lights a fire before the beacon at Tara is fired at dawn is punishable by death?

Patrick: (*calmly*) I am celebrating the festival of a still greater King than Laoghaire of Tara.

Lucatmael: Who can be a greater ruler than Laoghaire?

Patrick: Jesus of Nazareth.

Lucatmael: (*to 2nd Druid*) Have you heard of a king of that name?

2nd Druid: No.

Lucatmael: Whoever he is, his servant here is a cunning and impudent fellow. We must handle him carefully. Wait . . . I have a plan. (*Speaks to Patrick.*) The King invites you and your company to Tara as his guests. No doubt your reasons for lighting a flame on this holy night are excellent, and we will listen with interest to them. Tomorrow at a great banquet you will be welcome to address us. So come now with me and my companions, and we will see you safely to the King's hall at Tara. (*Aside to 2nd Druid*) Be sure the guards secure all escape routes.

Scene II: The Great Hall of Laoghaire, King of Tara.
King seated at table with 2 Druids.

Lucatmael: This cup, O King, holds the poison for the foreigner. This one is yours.

King: Good, good Lucatmael. Your plan of inviting him here was a clever one. You have the warriors hidden on the road to prevent his turning back?

Lucatmael: Yes, O King.

King: Good! Dubtach! Let's have one of your ballads. Sing with him, Fiacc. (*Dubtach starts to strum harp. Enter Patrick.*)

King: Welcome to Tara, beardless one.
  (*Patrick bows.*)

Voices (*from those standing around*): Who is this man? Why is he here? What is his purpose? Where does he come from?

Patrick: I have come with a message of peace.

2nd Druid: The man lies. He is here to spread treason against our king.

Voices: Treason! Who brought him here? Let him begone! Put him in chains!

Patrick: (*over the hubbub*) I have come not to speak treason, but to teach loyalty—loyalty to the spirit of God. There isn't a man among you who doesn't live in fear. Even now as you eat, each of you sits trembling under his shield! And what do you live in dread of? War! The continual, ruinous warfare of your own making. I have come to build schools, to educate your young, to teach you the law of love!

King: (*stands up*) These are strange words you speak. I do not pretend to understand your motives for lighting a fire against my orders. However, let us be friends. (*King picks up cups, holds out poisoned one to Patrick.*) We shall toast to our friendship.
  (*Patrick takes cup, carries it to his lips. Dubtach jumps up, snatches cup and hurls it to the floor; then stands amazed.*)

Dubtach: Sire, forgive my impudence. I know I stand in danger of my life for this action. But I have felt from the first that if we poison this man, we shall bring a calamity upon Ireland.

Fiacc: (*stands*) I agree with you. This stranger is our friend.

2nd Druid: You must be possessed thus to flout King Laoghaire, son of Niall of the Nine Hostages!

King: Silence! (*To Patrick*) What I have just witnessed makes it evident to me that you have entered my hall under the protection of a supernatural power. I am not going to dispute it by tampering with your life. We've had enough quarreling. Let's get on with the feast. Sit here by me. (*To others*) Bring more grilled trout for our guest, and a fresh cup of wine! (*To Patrick*) You can hardly be a menace to my throne if you go through the kingdom teaching the power of love.

Scene III: On the road to Cavan.

Captain: Now, men, you take up stations right here—one on each side of the path. The Druids say that Patrick is coming our way, and they don't want him disturbing everything the way he's done at Slane. So just you keep a good watch, and when he comes along, get him!

Guards: Yes sir. (*They crouch down behind two chairs. Captain leaves. Enter Patrick and two monks.*)

Patrick: We must go carefully, brothers, for there may be soldiers waiting to prevent us, and we want to be sure we bring the Gospel safely to Cavan.

1st Monk: Father Patrick, sing us that song the Lord gave you. When I hear it, our Saviour himself seems to be shielding us from harm.

2nd Monk: Yes, Father Patrick, teach us to sing it, too.

Patrick: All right, brothers. A bit of a song will help our feet over these hills, too. (*Sings first line of St. Patrick's Breastplate; see page 91. The others join in. As they sing they pass between the two guards.*)

1st Guard: Did you see that deer!

2nd Guard: Yes. What a beauty! How strange to see one right on the road.

1st Guard: And with two fawns, too. Strange!

Patrick and Monks: (*Sing more of song while exiting.*)

Captain: (*enters*) Ho, guards!

Guards: (*Jump up and salute.*) Sir!

Captain: No sign of Patrick yet?

1st Guard: Neither sign nor sound, sir.

Captain: Strange . . . I was certain he'd come by this road. He must have gone a different way . . . Well, it's nearly sundown. He won't come now. Let's get back to the garrison. (*They march off.*)

Narrator: The story that Patrick drove the snakes out of Ireland was not told until the 12th century; and then what was said was, "After Patrick there were no more Druids in Ireland, no sorcerers and no snakes."

Patrick's outstanding accomplishment was the founding of monasteries. Thousands of converts gathered at Bangor, Kells, and other towns in northern Ireland. Living in individual huts like hermits, they gathered for prayer and for study of the Scriptures, the Church Fathers, and classical authors. Part of their study took the form of copying manuscripts and illuminating them with beautiful capital letters embellished with exquisite paintings. One of the most famous manuscripts in the world—the Book of Kells—was produced at an Irish abbey.

Meanwhile, the very church in Europe that had been the instrument of Ireland's conversion was going down before the onslaught of paganism and social disorganization which we call the Dark Ages.

A century after Patrick lit the flame on the mountain of Slane, the Pope sent messengers to the monastery of Bangor, begging for volunteers to go as missionaries to Europe. Many Irish monks answered the call. In the 6th and 7th centuries hundreds of missionaries went forth from the monasteries of Ireland to preach the Gospel and set up new monasteries. They travelled southeast as far as Switzerland, Bavaria, and Italy, and west to Iceland and probably North America. Many of Europe's oldest monasteries date back to Irish foundations, though many later adopted the rule of St. Benedict. The Irish Church is credited with bringing much of Europe back to the Christian faith it had lost, laying the foundations for medieval Christianity.

St. Patrick's Breastplate

'Bunessan'

Words attributed to
St. Patrick

Gaelic Melody

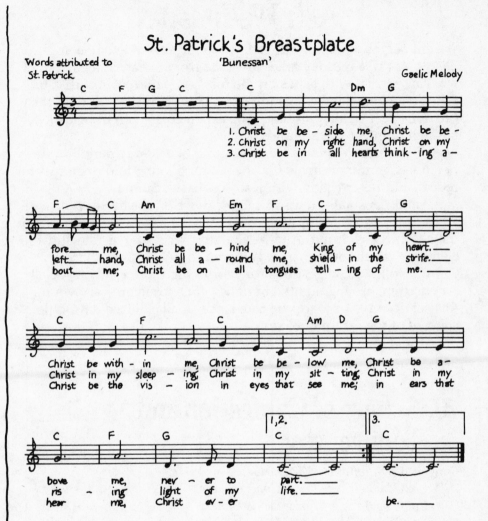

1. Christ be be-side me, Christ be be-fore___ me, Christ be be-hind me, King of my heart.___ Christ be with-in me, Christ be be-low me, Christ be a-bove me, nev-er to part.___

2. Christ on my right hand, Christ on my left___ hand, Christ all a-round me, shield in the strife.___ Christ in my sleep-ing, Christ in my sit-ting, Christ in my ris-ing, light of my life.___

3. Christ be in all hearts think-ing a-bout___ me; Christ be on all tongues tell-ing of me.___ Christ be the vis-ion in eyes that see me; in ears that hear me, Christ ev-er be.___

Translation ©1969, James Quinn, printed by permission of Geoffrey Chapman, a division of Cassell Ltd., 35 Red Lion Square, London WC1R 4SG England. From NEW HYMNS FOR ALL SEASONS by Fr. James Quinn, S.J., Geoffrey Chapman, London, 1969.

Ash Wednesday

Lent begins on Ash Wednesday, the fortieth weekday before Easter. Ash Wednesday takes its name from the ancient custom of marking a cross with ashes on the foreheads of the faithful. (The ashes may be made by burning dried palm branches used on the previous year's Palm Sunday.) The ashen cross is an outward, visible sign of inward repentance.

Ash Wednesday marks the beginning of a 40-day period of repentance, genuine sorrow for one's wrongdoing, and openness for rebirth and resurrection with Jesus on Easter Sunday.

A family or small-group worship service on the eve of Ash Wednesday can be composed of various components depending on the age of the children. A rather lengthy service, which includes elements which Linas Brown gathered for use at Reba Place Church, follows. Suggestions for shortening the service, especially for children, are highlighted in italics. If children are very young, this service may be inappropriate since small children have little concept of the meaning of sin.

70. Service of Confession and Forgiveness

Sing opening invitation: "Kumbaya"
> *Come by here, my Lord, Come by here.*
> *Come by here, my Lord, Come by here.*
> *Come by here, my Lord, Come by here.*
> *O Lord, Come by here.*

Read Old Testament Scripture: Joel 2:12–17 (for children, only verses 12–13).

Antiphonally read Psalm 103: 1–22:*

Bless the Lord, O my soul; and all that is within me, bless his holy name!
Bless the Lord, O my soul, and forget not all his benefits,
Who forgives all your iniquity,

Who heals all your diseases,
Who redeems your life from the pit,
Who crowns you with steadfast love and mercy,
Who satisfies you with good as long as you live so that your youth is renewed like the eagle's.
The Lord works vindication and justice for all who are oppressed.
He made known his ways to Moses, his acts to the people of Israel.
The Lord is merciful and gracious, slow to anger and abounding in steadfast love.
He will not always chide, nor will he keep his anger for ever.
He does not deal with us according to our sins, nor requite us according to our iniquities.
For as the Heavens are high above the earth, so great is his steadfast love toward those who fear him:
As far as the east is from the west, so far does he remove our transgressions from us.
As a father pities his children, so the Lord pities those who fear him.
For he knows our frame; he remembers that we are dust.
As for man, his days are like grass; he flourishes like a flower of the field;
For the wind passes over it, and it is gone, and its place knows it no more.
But the steadfast love of the Lord is from everlasting to everlasting upon those who fear him.
And his righteousness to children's children.
To those who keep his covenant and remember to do his commandments.
The Lord has established his throne in the heavens, and his kingdom rules over all.
Bless the Lord, O you his angels, you mighty ones who do his word, hearkening to the voice of his word!
Bless the Lord, all his hosts, his ministers that do his will!
Bless the Lord, all his works, in all places of his dominion.
Bless the Lord, O my soul!

Sing Isaac Watts hymn, "O Bless the Lord, My Soul," from Psalm 103.

Leader explains the significance of the cross of ashes:
I will put a cross made of ashes on your forehead as an outward sign of your inner sorrow for the wrong that you do and the hurt that you cause others. Jesus' death on the cross made it possible for you to be forgiven.

(Continued)

All who care to participate, kneel, while the leader marks each with the ashen sign of the cross saying:
   Remember that you are dust and to dust you shall return.

Someone in turn marks the leader's forehead.

While kneeling pray together: Psalm 51:1–17 (for children verses 7-12).

(If available, the Litany of Penitence from The Book of Common Prayer can be added here.)

Leader reads: "If we confess our sins, he is faithful and just and will forgive us our sins and purify us from all unrighteousness." (I John 1:9).
   "For God so loved the world that he gave his one and only Son, that whoever believes in him shall not perish but have eternal life." (John 3:16).

All rise and embrace each other.

Leader says: As a sign of the Lord's forgiveness, remove the ashes from each other's foreheads.

Sing: "Jesus, Priceless Treasure"

*See note on page 32 about use of inclusive language.

Lent

"Lent" is a term derived from Anglo-Saxon, meaning "long days" or "spring." It dates from the 4th century and was a time of special discipline for those who were to be baptized on Easter. In time, it became a spring period of fasting and penitence for all, in preparation for Easter.

Lent is a season of death and rising. Traditionally it is a season for expressing death to one's self by giving up something beyond what one normally gives up. Death to self can also be expressed by an intentional giving to others. With careful thought ahead of time, the Lenten season can give rise to a family plan of action—acts of love toward family members and/or acts of love that extend to others beyond the family circle.

71. Focusing on Others' Suffering and Jesus' Ministry

Hilda Carper suggests that Lent is the season to focus on needs and suffering in the larger world. One could prepare a bulletin board with pictures of people from around the world. Using pertinent books or movies for family worship time that focus on suffering that others endure could be a significant way of opening children's consciousness to greater human need.

Lent is also a good time to focus on Jesus' ministry after Christmas and leading up to Easter. Family devotions could center on the stories of Jesus' boyhood, baptism and teaching/healing ministry.

For a family memorization project, Lent would be an excellent time to memorize the Sermon on the Mount, Matthew 5:3-12, a verse every day or so. Another timely scripture for reading or memorizing would be Matthew 25:31-46 where Jesus says, "I tell you the truth, whatever you did for one of the least of these brothers of mine, you did for me."

72. A Family Pledge to "Do Without"

At the beginning of Lent, the Shuford family has a meeting to discuss what it is each of them will pledge to do without for the Lenten season. One year, one of the children decided to do without television after school for the duration of the 40 days. Another decided to give up an afternoon snack and another, chewing gum. One of the parents pledged to do without any between-meal snacks and another to go without second helpings of food. The Shufords use these small sacrifices as reminders throughout Lent of Jesus' large sacrifice. (Parents should help children choose a "sacrifice" that is manageable and age-appropriate.)

When the entire family joins in this discipline together, a sense of solidarity heightens each person's resolve to carry on. Care is needed in eliciting the participation of the children so that they will *want* to join in on a common family project and won't feel forced to cooperate. It is a challenge—"Are you willing to try this with me?"—not a new law.

Children learn that indeed they can restrain their desires. They learn that a great deal of satisfaction can come with being faithful to one's commitment. And above all, while exercising this discipline, they may begin to understand that their deepest need is not for more things, but for God.

73. A Wheat Seed Parable of "Dying to Self"

The Ewing family acts out a little parable of "dying to oneself" during Lent, based on Jesus' statement, "I tell you the truth, unless a kernel of wheat falls to the ground and dies, it remains only a single seed. But if it dies, it produces many seeds" (John 12:24).

The Ewings set a pot of dirt and a cup of wheat seeds in a central location. For every kind deed one person does for another, he or she may plant a seed, pushing it into the ground with a finger. Wheat seeds only take a week or so to sprout. If all goes well, the pot will soon display a promising mini-crop of wheat.

74. Lenten Love Projects

The Ewings also embark on a "Lenten Journey of Love" beginning six weeks before Easter. The Ewings got the idea from a little book entitled *The Celebration Book*. In order to enhance their sharing of love, the Ewings do a "love project" each week of Lent.

First Week: "The hand of love." Write a letter a day to someone, saying how much you appreciate them.

Second Week: "The voice of love." Telephone someone each day to encourage, thank, forgive, or express love.

Third Week: "The deed of love." Take a simple gift to two or three people, homemade, child-made, flowers, etc.

Fourth Week: "The heart of love." Make a list of five people for whom you will pray daily. Include both friends and enemies. Forgive them if they have wronged you. Ask forgiveness if you have wronged them.

Fifth Week: "The mind of love." Use this week to pray for yourself and to look inward. Praise God for God's love whether you find yourself in the heights or in the depths.

Sixth Week: "The victory of love." This is the week of celebration. Thank God for God's love revealed in many ways. Rejoice that Christ lives. Get outdoors and enjoy the new life in God's creation.

Palm Sunday

75. Palm Branches and Songs

Any reenactment of the crowds and "hosannas" that accompanied Jesus as he entered Jerusalem on a donkey would best happen in a large congregation. However, if that isn't possible, the crowd fervor can still be symbolically commemorated in a smaller family gathering.

Read the story of Jesus' triumphal entry into Jerusalem: Matthew 21:1-11; Luke 19:37-40. Spend a lengthy time in spirited singing. Two songs used at a Reba Place Palm Sunday celebration are included below. "Hosanna, Son of David" serves as a rousing musical chant in the Reba Place Palm Sunday drama. As "Jesus" is wheeled in on a "donkey," the congregation surges around him, waving palms. One can begin to sense the elation and joyful relief of the crowd in Jerusalem as they welcomed their long-awaited Deliverer. Any favorite praise songs could be used as you walk around and around, waving palm branches, and praising God for the King who "comes to you, gentle and riding on a donkey."

Following the singing, you may want to sit down again and read several more scriptures that will help to set the stage for the upcoming events of Holy Week: Matthew 21:12-17, 21:23-27, 26:1-13.

Hosanna, Son of David

Marcia Lind

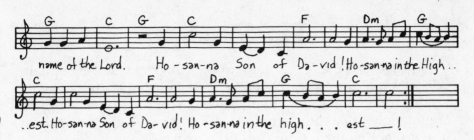

name of the Lord. Ho-san-na Son of Da-vid! Ho-san-na in the High..

..est. Ho-san-na Son of Da-vid! Ho-san-na in the high . . . est ___ !

© 1975 by Reba Place Church.

'Sanna

Traditional
Arr. Betty Pulkingham

With fervency of expression

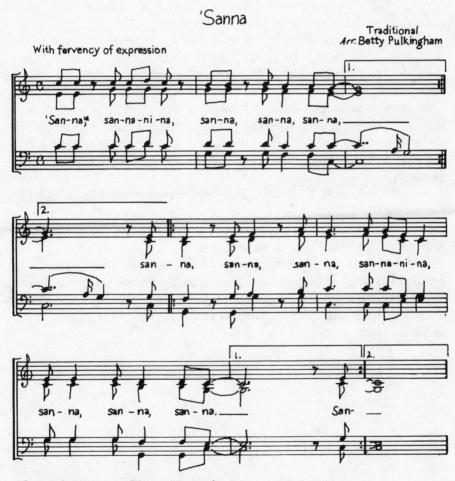

'San-na,* san-na-ni-na, san-na, san-na, san-na, _____

san — na, san-na, san — na, san-na-ni-na,

san — na, san — na, san — na. _____ San- —

*This is a shortened form of the word 'hosanna.'

This song may be sung most effectively by voices in four-part harmony, unaccompanied.

The Passover

In Jesus' day, the Jewish feast of the Passover was the annual celebration of the greatest event in Jewish sacred history—the exodus from bondage in Egypt. The night of the Passover was that fateful night in Egypt when the death angel passed over the Israelites, exempting them from God's divine wrath. On that night, God delivered them from the power of Pharoah and freed them from slavery. Passover became the first feast celebrated by the Jewish nation.

Passover is celebrated in the spring and frequently coincides with the Easter holidays. Jesus celebrated the Passover with his disciples, his "last supper" with them before his trial and crucifixion.

Many folks at Reba Place celebrate an adaptation of the traditional Passover Seder. Entering into the commemoration of this pivotal event in Judeo-Christian history has heightened our appreciation of the heritage that is the cradle of our faith and subsequent salvation.

A Passover service adapted from several that have been used at Reba Place is included below. Parents with very small children may want to select and use only portions of the service. Specify ahead of time which child is to read which part.

Seder means "order." The order of the service takes place around the dinner table before and after the meal. Individuals take turns reading from the *Haggadah*, "the telling." The Exodus story is told, questions are asked, symbols from the seder plate are explained and songs are sung.

76. How to Set the Seder Table

The ceremonial Seder plate, whose symbols are explained during the service, is arranged and set in the center of the table. It should look like this:

1. **The charred lamb bone:** represents the sacrifice of the Paschal lamb.

2. **Haroset:** a mixture of equal parts of grated apple and chopped nuts mixed with a little honey, cinnamon and wine. It resembles the mortar used by the Israelites in Egypt. Its sweetness symbolizes the hope of freedom.

3. **Ground horseradish:** bitter herbs symbolizing the Jews' bitter suffering in Egypt.

4. **Parsley:** an old form of hors d'oeuvres symbolizing life. It is later dipped in salt water as a reminder of the tears shed in slavery.

5. **Roasted egg:** symbolizes the free-will offering brought to the temple on all festivals.

Also set on the table:

1. A pitcher of wine or grape juice (as your family chooses); juice glasses at everyone's place.

2. Extra bowls of horseradish, haroset and parsley for passing at the appropriate times (if the table is large and not all can reach the Sedar plate).

3. A bowl of salt water into which the parsley will be dipped.

4. A plate with three matzahs (unleavened bread which can be purchased).

5. An empty chair and an empty cup, to signify the Cup of Elijah, which is filled toward the end of the meal in hope that the prophet Elijah may appear, as a messenger of the Almighty, sent to announce the coming of the Messiah. (Since Christians believe the Messiah has already come you may want to substitute "Christ" for "Elijah" in the reading.)

6. Candles and flowers, as desired.

77. The Order of the Passover Service (Haggadah)*

Child: Today we celebrate the Passover meal. Let us begin by lighting the festival candles. *(Mother lights candles.)*

All: Blessed art thou, O Lord our God, King of the Universe, who hast sanctified us by Thy word. In your honor we kindle the lights of the holiday.

Father: *(pours first goblet of juice)* Let us praise the name of the Lord and proclaim His greatness to all generations, for He delivered His people from bondage. He has given us anniversaries for rejoicing, festivals and seasons for gladness. This Passover, the season of our freedom, is a memorial of our departure from Egypt. Blessed be His name. As we lift up this cup of wine, let us welcome the festival of Passover and rejoice in the joy of our salvation.

Mother: *(passes pitcher and all pour juice into goblets)* Wine is a traditional Jewish symbol of joy. Years ago our fathers and mothers would squeeze the juice out of grapes that grew on ther vines and prepare wine for the holiday. It was the sweetest thing they knew and showed how happy the festival made them.

All: Blessed art thou, O Lord our God, King of the Universe, who created the fruit of the vine. *(All drink juice.)*

Child: Why is this night different from all other nights?

Father: I am glad you asked this question, for the story of this night is just what I wanted you to know. Indeed, this night is different from all other nights for on this night we celebrate the going forth of the Hebrew people from slavery into freedom. If the Holy One, blessed be He, had not brought our fathers and mothers out from Egypt, then we and our children, and our children's children, would be slaves of Pharaoh. But the mighty arm of the Lord delivered us. Therefore, it is our desire to tell the story again and again of our coming forth from Egypt.

All Sing: When Israel was in Egypt Land,
    Let my people go.
    Oppressed so hard they could not stand.
    Let my people go.
    Go down, Moses,
    Way down in Egypt Land,

Tell old Pharaoh,
Let my people go!
(If time permits read Exodus 12:1-14, 17, 21-36.)

Mother: *(Breaks matzah from matzah plate. Passes it around and all take a piece.)* This is the Bread of Affliction which our mothers and fathers ate in the land of Egypt. Let all who are needy come celebrate the redemption of God.

All: Blessed art thou, O Lord our God, King of the Universe who brings forth bread from the earth. *(All eat matzah.)*

Child: Why do we eat only unleavened bread tonight?

Father: When Pharaoh let our mothers and fathers go from Egypt they were forced to flee in great haste. They had no time to bake their bread. They could not wait for the yeast to rise. So the sun, beating down on the dough as they carried it along, baked it into a flat, unleavened bread called matzah.

Child: Why do we eat bitter herbs tonight?

Mother: *(Everyone tastes the horseradish.)* We eat bitter herbs because our mothers and fathers were slaves in Egypt and their lives were made bitter.

Child: Why do we sip the herb in salt water?

Father: *(Everyone dips parsley in salt water and eats.)* We dip parsley into salt water because salt water reminds us of the tears the Israelites shed while in slavery.

Child: Why do we mix the bitter herbs with the sweet haroset?

Mother: *(All mix a little horseradish and haroset on their own plates and eat.)* We eat the bitter herbs with the sweet haroset as a sign of hope. Our mothers and fathers were able to withstand the bitterness of slavery because it was sweetened by the hope of freedom.

Child: Why do we lay back and relax at the table?

Father: *(All visibly relax.)* In olden times reclining at the table was a sign of a free person. Since our mothers and fathers were freed on this night, we recline at the table.

Child: What does the lamb bone on the plate symbolize?

Mother: The lamb bone reminds us of the lamb that was sacrificed, the blood on the door, and that the Lord passed over our homes when He visited death upon the Egyptians.

Child: And the egg, what does that mean?

Father: The egg is a symbol of new life. It was brought as a free-will offering to the temple on all festivals.

Father: We have been instructed well. Therefore, let us praise, glorify, exult, honor, bless and adore Him who performed for our fathers and mothers and for us, all of these wonders. He brought us forth from slavery to freedom, from anguish to joy, from darkness to great light and from bondage to redemption. Let us sing therefore, before Him, a new song.

(Sing a song of praise, perhaps "I Will Sing of the Mercies of the Lord Forever" or "Great is Thy Faithfulness.")

All: Let the name of the Lord be blessed from this time forth and for evermore. From the rising of the sun until the going down thereof, the Lord's name is to be praised. The Lord is high above all nations, and His glory above the heavens. Who is like unto the Lord our God, that dwelleth so high; that looketh down so low upon the heavens and earth! He raiseth up the lowly out of the dust, and lifteth up the needy from the dunghill, that He may set him with princes, even with the princes of the people. He maketh the barren woman to dwell in her house as a joyful mother of children. Praise ye the Lord.

(All fill cups with juice or wine and drink a second time.)

(The sharing of a meal then follows.)

(After meal all fill cups with juice or wine a third time.)

Child: Why do we have an empty chair and an empty cup at the table?

Mother: Because we pray for the spirit of Elijah *(or substitute "Christ")* to enter this home and renew our hope. May war come to an end and all people live in peace. May our hearts be united in the Lord's service and our lives sanctified by His will. *(Pour juice into Elijah's cup and all drink from individual cups.)*

All: Blessed be our God. By His great goodness we have been supplied in abundance.

Father: How can I repay unto the Lord all His bountiful dealings toward me?

All: I will lift up the cup of salvation and call upon the name of the Lord.

Mother: My vows I pay unto the Lord, yea, in the presence of all His people.

All: Precious in the sight of the Lord is the death of His saints.

Father: I beseech Thee, O Lord, for I am Thy servant, I am Thy servant, the son of Thy handmaid; Thou hast loosed my bonds.

All: I will offer to Thee the sacrifice of thanksgiving and will call upon the name of the Lord.

Mother: I will pay my vows to the Lord, yea, in the presence of all His people.

All: In the courts of the Lord's house, in the midst of thee, O Jerusalem. Hallelujah!

(All drink a fourth time from the cup of juice or wine.)

All: O praise the Lord, all ye nations; laud Him, all ye peoples. For His mercy is great toward us, and the truth of the Lord endureth forever. Hallelujah!

All: May the Lord bless us and keep us.
   May the Lord cause the light of His face to shine upon us, and be gracious unto us.
   May the Lord lift up His countenance upon us and give us peace.
   Next year in Jerusalem! Amen.

See note on page 32 about use of inclusive language.

Maundy Thursday

The Love Feast, practiced in some church circles on the Thursday evening of Holy Week, is a beautiful and meaningful tradition. However, since children are often excluded from the communion service that accompanies the meal, they are seldom able to experience the drama of the Last Supper.

Our focus in this collection of celebrations is on worship activities based in the home. The intent is to find ways to include children in the rich experience of the family of God.

Maundy Thursday is a lovely time to include children in re-enacting the events of Jesus' last supper with his friends. Children's participation, on their own level of understanding in a short, home-based dramatization of the Last Supper, is very appropriate. (Parents may want to explain to the younger children that at an older age they will grow to understand more fully what Jesus' words mean and that then they will be able to participate in a church-based communion service.)

The following service could be enacted before or after a simple evening meal of bread and soup.

78. A Family Reenactment of Jesus' Last Supper

Father: It was just before the Passover Feast. Jesus knew the time had come for him to leave this world and go to the Father. He had always loved those who were his in the world, but now he showed them the full extent of his love.

Mother: The evening meal was being served. Judas Iscariot had already made arrangements to betray Jesus. Jesus knew that God the Father had put all things under his, Jesus', power, and that he had come from God and was returning to God.

Father: So Jesus got up from the meal, removed his garment and wrapped a towel around his waist. He poured water into a basin and began to wash his disciples' feet, drying them with the towel that was wrapped around him.

(Father gets up and wraps a towel around his waist. He pours water into a basin and moves to the eldest child. Father waits.)

Mother: Jesus came to Simon Peter, who said to him,

Eldest Child: "Lord, are you going to wash my feet?"

Father: Jesus replied, "You do not realize now what I am doing, but later you will understand."

Eldest Child: "No," said Peter, "you shall never wash my feet."

Father: Jesus answered, "Unless I wash you, you have no part with me."

Eldest Child: "Then, Lord, not just my feet but my hands and my head as well!"

Father: Jesus answered, "A person who has had a bath needs only to wash his feet; his whole body is clean. And you are clean, though not every one of you."

Mother: Jesus knew who was going to betray him, and that was why he said that not everyone was clean.

(Father proceeds to wash feet of eldest child, embracing him or her as he finishes. Then the eldest child washes the next person's feet and on around the circle until the last person washes the Father's feet. The family may want to sing or listen to music during the washing.)

Father: When Jesus had finished washing their feet, he put on his clothes and returned to his place. "Do you understand what I have done for you?" he asked them. "Now that I, your Lord and Teacher, have washed your feet, you also should wash one another's feet. I have set you an example that you should do as I have done for you. Now that you know these things, you will be blessed if you do them."

Mother: While they were eating, Jesus took bread, gave thanks and broke it, and gave it to his disciples, saying, "Take it; this is my body."

(Pass bread around the table; everyone break off a piece and eat.)

Father: Then Jesus took the cup and gave thanks. He said, "This is my blood of the covenant, which is poured out for many. I tell you the truth, I will not drink again of the fruit of the vine until that day when I drink it anew in the kingdom of God." He offered the cup to them and they all drank.

(Continued)

(Pass a cup of grape juice around the table; everyone take a sip. Sing a hymn together.)

Father: Jesus said, "My children, I will be with you only a little longer. You will look for me, and just as I told the Jews, so I tell you now: where I am going, you cannot come." Jesus continued, "A new commandment I give you: Love one another. As I have loved you, so you must love one another. All people will know that you are my disciples if you love one another."

2nd Child: Simon Peter asked Jesus, "Lord, where are you going?"

Mother: Jesus replied, "Where I am going, you cannot follow now, but you will follow later."

2nd Child: Peter asked, "Lord, why can't I follow you now? I will lay down my life for you."

Father: Then Jesus answered, "Will you really lay down your life for me? I tell you the truth: before this rooster crows, you will disown me three times!"

Mother: Jesus comforted his disciples, saying, "Do not let your hearts be troubled. Trust in God; trust also in me. In my Father's house are many rooms; if it were not so, I would have told you. I am going there to prepare a place for you. And if I go and prepare a place for you, I will come back and take you to be with me that you also may be where I am. You know the way to the place where I am going."

3rd Child: Thomas said to Jesus, "Lord, we don't know where you are going, so how can we know the way?"

Father: Jesus answered, "I am the way and the truth and the life. No one comes to the Father except through me. If you really knew me, you would know my Father as well. From now on, you do know him and have seen him."

4th Child: Philip said, "Lord, show us the Father and that will be enough for us."

Mother: Jesus answered, "Don't you know me, Philip, even after I have been among you such a long time? Anyone who has seen me has seen the Father."

(Close by praying the Lord's Prayer together, holding hands around the table.)

Good Friday Commemoration

The Good Friday service below is adapted from the traditional Catholic stations of the cross. A family may choose to participate in walking the way of the cross at a Catholic Church. However, another way of entering into the pathos of Jesus' suffering and death could be a "Reader's Theater."

Participants sit around a table and take turns reading the passages of scripture suggested below. All lights are turned off except for seven black candles which are lit on the table. As the readings suggested below progress, the candles are blown out, one at a time, until all are extinguished. (There are 14 scriptures so a candle could be blown out after each second scripture.)

This service, because of its sadness and pain, is likely inappropriate for small children. Parents could choose to read parts of the story in Mark 14:32-15:47 and perhaps sit only momentarily in darkness before reminding small children that Christ did indeed rise from the dead and lives even now.

At the end of the service below, there are two alternatives suggested. After the candles are all blown out, you may choose to sit in darkness for awhile and then disband; or, you may want to turn on a low light, read the final suggested scripture and sing together.

79. Good Friday Reader's Theater

1. Jesus is condemned to death.
   Read Matthew 27:11-26
2. Jesus accepts his cross.
   Read Mark 15:16-20
3. Jesus falls the first time.
   Read Psalm 5
4. Jesus meets his mother.
   Read Luke 2:25-35

5. Simon helps Jesus.
   Read Matthew 27:32

6. Veronica wipes the face of Jesus.
   Read Isaiah 53:4-5

7. Jesus falls the second time.
   Read Acts 3:17-26

8. Jesus consoles the women.
   Read Luke 23:27-31

9. Jesus falls the third time.
   Read Isaiah 53:7-9

10. Jesus is stripped of his garments.
    Read John 19:23-24

11. Jesus is nailed to the cross.
    Read Mark 15:22-36

12. Jesus dies on the cross.
    Read John 19:25-30

13. Jesus is placed in the arms of his mother.
    Read John 19:31-37

14. Jesus is buried in the tomb.
    Read John 19:38-42

Sit silently in darkness.

Disband, or light a low light. As a statement of faith read together John 11:25-26.

Sing together: "What Wondrous Love Is This?"
　　　　　　　　 "Were You There" (first three verses)

80. Good Friday Prayer Vigil

Reba Place Church holds a prayer vigil every year which lasts from Maundy Thursday's Love Feast until the Good Friday evening service.

Susanne Coalson explains that an invitation is given for volunteers who want to "watch with the Lord for one hour" to choose a slot of time in that 24-hour period to come to the prayer room and pray. Prayer requests are drawn up and kept in an open notebook that stays in the prayer room during the vigil. The idea is to focus on special prayer concerns as a whole church. But even more fundamental is the belief that it is good to spend time in prayer, especially during the memorial of our Lord's suffering.

The story of Jesus' arrest in the Garden is available in the prayer room, as is the above mentioned prayer notebook in which persons write additional prayer requests or words of new insight as they feel led to do so. A kneeling bench adds comfort for those who choose to pray for long periods of time.

A family may want to keep a prayer vigil. It isn't likely that there will be enough participants to keep a continual prayer chain going. But a place of prayer—a small room, closet, or corner—could be made inviting with a candle, kneeling bench and prayer books. The understanding within a family context could be that, as often as possible, family members will return to the prayer room to "watch with Jesus" during the memorial of his trial and death.

Easter Traditions

81. A Traditional Easter Greeting

If a family has taken time to enter into the darkness and despair that the friends of Jesus felt at his death, the news of Jesus' resurrection will be welcome indeed. On Easter morning, instead of greeting one another with a standard "Good morning," use the traditional Orthodox affirmation:

"The Lord is risen!"

Response: "He is risen indeed!"

At the breakfast table, read one of the Gospel accounts of the Easter story, light a large new candle and sing an Easter carol.

82. An Easter Breakfast of Armenian Pastry

Easter morning breakfast is a lovely time for a special touch—a new pastry, hot cross buns, hot chocolate—a surprise that greets all on rising or on returning from a sunrise service. The Vogt family picked up an Armenian tradition of small baked goodies made in unusual shapes called Cheoreg (see recipe below). Easter dinner in their home always included a cake in the shape of a lamb.

Cheoreg

Children can easily take part in the preparation of this pastry, particularly in cutting out shapes from the rolled dough.

3½ cups flour	1 tsp. yeast
¼ cup sugar	⅓ cup + 1 Tbsp. warm milk
½ tsp. salt	1 egg
½ cup real butter	egg yolk
½ cup shortening	poppy or sesame seeds

Cut butter and shortening into flour, sugar and salt. Take teaspoon of yeast and dissolve in a little water. Mix warm milk and egg with the softened yeast. Mix in flour/butter mixture. Let rise for several hours.

Roll out dough to ½-inch thickness. Cut in shapes with cookie cutters. Brush with beaten egg yolk. Sprinkle with poppy or sesame seeds. Let rise again. Bake at 350 degrees for 10 minutes.

Serve with fruit and cheese platter.

83. Making an Egg Tree

A tradition in Brigitte Krummel's home is making an egg tree. The insides of eggs are blown out after puncturing a pinhole in each end of each egg. The dried, clean eggs can then be painted, often in intricate designs. The eggs are saved from year to year and more are added as time goes on. The painted eggs are hung with narrow ribbons on an "egg tree," a bare, budding branch which is placed in a pot in the middle of the table the day before Easter.

84. Easter Baskets

Children's Easter baskets are a tradition in several Reba Place homes. Each child has a basket which is lined with moss. A parent fills the basket with goodies the night before Easter and hides each in a different place. The kids look all over the house for their baskets first thing Easter morning.

85. Sending Off Balloons

A Reba Place tradition, following the Easter church celebration, is for the whole congregation to walk with helium-filled, brightly colored balloons to the Lake Michigan beach. A card with an Easter greeting and the sender's name and address is attached to a bundle of four or more balloons. (The more balloons tied together the greater the lift.) Everyone releases the balloons together while singing an Easter carol such as "Alleluia, Sing to Jesus" or "Lift Your Glad Voices."

The rising chorus of balloons and voices symbolically expresses the whole congregation's desire to share the good news of the resurrection. A family may want to participate in a balloon launch on a smaller scale.

Mother's Day and Father's Day

86. A Meal in Mom's or Dad's Honor

On their respective days, Mom and Dad are usually deserving of some extra special attention. One suggestion from the Shenk home is for Mom or Dad to be served their choice of breakfast (in bed if they desire), or their choice of dinner. The children are encouraged to write a love note or to make a small gift (if they haven't spontaneously done so already) to give at the meal.

Talk at the meal includes ways the honored parent has helped to make home and family a pleasant place to belong. The parent reflects on why he or she likes being a father or a mother and on the areas in which he or she would like to do better.

Finally, all gather around the celebrated parent and place hands on him or her as a sign of unity and affection. Each prays for the parent, thanking God and asking God's blessing on father and husband, on mother and wife.

The parent then responds with these words:

My son [my daughter], keep your father's commands
    and do not forsake your mother's teaching.
Bind them upon your heart forever;
    fasten them around your neck.
When you walk, they will guide you;
    when you sleep, they will watch over you;
    when you awake, they will speak to you.
For these commands are a lamp,
    this teaching is a light. (Proverbs 6:20-23a)

114

Jewish Feast of Shavuot

Sara Ewing, whose childhood home was Jewish, recalls her family's celebration of Shavuot (sha-vu-ot).

Seven weeks after Passover was a time for Jews to gather in Jerusalem to express their thanks and dependence upon God during the Feast of Shavuot. The Greek translation of the word is "Pentecost," meaning "fifty" because Shavuot falls 50 days (or seven weeks) after the Passover.

Shavuot means "feast of weeks" (Exodus 34:22, Deuteronomy 16:10). Other names in the scriptures for the holiday are "day of first fruits" (Numbers 28:26, Leviticus 23:15-17) and the "harvest feast" (Exodus 23:16). Rabbinic tradition points to Exodus 19:1 and says that God chose to be revealed on Mt. Sinai and gave the Law to Moses on Shavuot.

Shavuot is an "old covenant" holiday, Sara explains, but it has many "new covenant" counterparts:

1. Old covenant: giving of the law
   New covenant: giving of the Holy Spirit (II Corinthians 3:6-11)
2. Old covenant: thanksgiving for first harvest
   New covenant: beginning of the "harvest" of those redeemed
   in Christ
3. Old covenant: the commissioning of a nation to represent
   God (Exodus 19:6)
   New covenant: the birth of the church to represent God (I Peter 2:9, 10)

87. How to Celebrate Shavuot

1. Decorate the home with greens and flowers because Sinai was green when the Law was given.
2. Before the evening meal or at another convenient time, read or tell the biblical story of Ruth to the children. The Ruth story is significant because the events of the book took place during the first harvest of the year. Ruth is also significant because she, as a Moabite and an outsider, freely chose to adopt the Jewish faith and to live by the Jewish Law.
3. Have different family members read pre-arranged verses:

a) about the goodness of following God's Word—Proverbs 30:5, Isaiah 40:8, Hebrews 4:12;
b) about the goodness of the law being written in our hearts by the Spirit—Jeremiah 31:31-33, II Corinthians 3:6-11, Galatians 3:10-14, Romans 8:23.

4. For the meal eat dairy products like blintzes, cheesecake or noodle kugel. The Law is compared to milk and honey. Tradition says that the people were too tired after receiving the Law to kosher meat.

5. Serve two small loaves of bread, known as "hallot," during the meal. In the Old Testament two loaves were offered in the temple to represent the two tablets of the Law.

6. Following the meal gather together a bag of food stuffs, symbolic of some of the first harvest fruits, to give to the poor. In Ruth, the harvesters left some stalks of grain behind in the field for the poor to glean. Take the food to a local shelter for the homeless or some other relief agency.

Pentecost

Pentecost, in recent years, has been the occasion for Christians to come together to pray for peace. It seems especially appropriate, on the commemoration of the outpouring of the Spirit on people gathered from many nations, to pray for the conversion of all hearts from trust in weapons of violence to faith in the God of peace.

88. A Family Peace Prayer Service

For a family prayer time focused on the desire for world peace,
the short readings below may be helpful. They are excerpted from
a "walk for peace" service prepared by Allan Howe, in which Reba
Place folks participated.

Opening Prayer

Leader: We join together with all those around the world who pray
for peace.

All: Grant us peace, Thy most precious gift, O Thou eternal source
of peace, and enable us to be its messenger unto the peoples of the
earth. Bless all countries, that all may ever be strongholds only of
peace and its advocate in the council of nations. May contentment
reign within all borders, health and happiness within all homes.
Strengthen the bonds of friendship and fellowship among all the
inhabitants of all lands. Thus will the love of Thy name hallow
every home and every heart. Praised be Thou, O Lord, Giver of
peace, whose name is Peace, whose commandment is Peace, the
seal of all whose blessings is Peace. Amen.

—*Rabbi Herbert Bronstein*

Corporate Prayer

Leader: From the paper and the news we know: Peace on our earth is
threatened.
Fear spreads abroad.
More and more lethal weapons are produced;
more and more costly raw materials are used for them;
more and more money is used for them;
less and less people are content.
In this situation we lay hold of God's word. It is hope and
light for us.
The prophet Isaiah saw the coming Peace in this way:
"The peoples will beat their swords into plowshares
and their spears into pruning hooks.
For nation shall not lift up sword against nation,
neither shall they learn war any more" (Isaiah 2:4).
We pray: God of peace, we ask you,
Make us into the materials of your peace.

(Continued)

Strengthen our resolve to do everything in our power for
peace.

Let the politicians sense our desire for peace,
so that they will not become tired of struggling for peace.

Let the peoples not lose the dream of a peaceful world free
of violence.

Amen.

—*Gotthard Preisser*

Responsive Prayers

Leader: Let us pray: Lord our God, all of humankind is longing for
peace. But this season is also filled with discord.

All: In (*name areas of discord and suffering from the daily news*).

Leader: O God of all peace, deliver your children from violence and
militarism.

All: And deliver us, O God, for we contribute to the fact that fear,
retaliation and violence again and again gain influence.

Leader: Let us confess more courageously, believe more joyously,
love more fervently.

All: Lord, give us a new beginning and give the world peace.
Amen.

89. A Pentecost Service of Many Tongues and Peoples

If different members of the family know a variety of languages
the following short service, prepared by Julius Belser, could be
used; or, instead of repeating the prayer in several languages, repeat it in English in response to the naming of different countries
familiar to the family.

Reader: Read Acts 2:1-8.

Leader: One of the gifts of the Spirit on Pentecost was the ability to
communicate the mighty works of God across language and cultural barriers. Some of us in this family have learned of other languages and cultures. In many areas of the world represented by
these different languages there are conflicts and urgent needs for

the Holy Spirit's power and blessing. In many places it is dangerous to speak God's word.

Let us join in the same prayer the early Christians prayed:

All: Now Lord, enable your Servants to speak your word with great
boldness. Stretch out your hand to heal and perform miraculous
signs and wonders through the name of your Holy Servant Jesus.
Acts 4:29,30

Leader: Now, as I mention various peoples around the world let us
pray for the Lord to pour out his Spirit upon them. (*Substitute
names of countries familiar to the family for the ones listed below. If different languages are known have individuals pray the Acts prayer in their
language; otherwise simply repeat the prayer in English as individuals or
as a group.*)

> Let us pray for the Arab and Jewish peoples of the Mid-
> East . . .
> > (*repeat the prayer shown above*)
>
> Let us pray for the people of the Soviet Union . . .
> > (*repeat prayer*)
>
> Let us pray the Spirit's blessing on the people in Yugoslavia
> and the other Eastern European nations . . .
> > (*repeat prayer*)
>
> Le us pray for renewal of the Christians in Sweden and in
> Western Europe . . .
> > (*repeat prayer*)
>
> Let us pray for the pouring out of God's renewing and recon-
> ciling Spirit in Zaire and the nations of Africa . . .
> > (*repeat prayer*)
>
> Let us ask God for the Spirit's gift for our brothers and sisters
> in India and the other Asian nations . . .
> > (*repeat prayer*)
>
> Let us pray for the peoples of Cambodia and the other nations
> of Southeast Asia . . .
> > (*repeat prayer*)
>
> Let us pray for the struggling peoples of El Salvador and the
> other Central and South American nations . . .
> > (*repeat prayer*)

Leader: After they prayed, the place where they were meeting was
shaken. And they were all filled with the Holy Spirit and spoke the
word of God boldly. Acts 4:31.

(Continued)

All: Sing to the Lord, praise his name; proclaim his salvation day after day. Declare his glory among the nations, his marvelous deeds among all peoples. For great is the Lord and most worthy of praise. Praise the name of the Lord. Amen.

90. A Kite for the Wind

As a Pentecost family project, make a kite or two using brilliant colors. Hilda Carper reports that the folks at Reba Place used to have a competition to see who could make the biggest and prettiest kite.

Take the kites out to a breezy meadow on Pentecost, if possible, for a lesson in the life of the Spirit: "The wind blows wherever it pleases. You hear its sound, but you cannot tell where it comes from or where it is going. So it is with everyone born of the Spirit." John 3:8.

91. A Poem of the Spirit

Susanne Coalson wrote a poem highlighting several qualities of the Spirit. Read it as a family and discuss how God's Spirit is like wind, water, light, life and love.

Portrait of Pentecost

It is so fresh
And so free
That they called it
    Wind—
A mighty, rushing wind.

It is so clean

And so full of health
That they called it
   Water—
A deep, gushing, never-failing spring.

It is so pure
And so radiant
That they called it
   Light—
Warm, purifying, living light.

It is so vital
And so powerful
That they called it
   Life—
The life that bursts open
Everything which tries to confine it—
Even death.

It is so gentle
And so intimate
That they called it
   Love—
In love, all that is good and holy
Draws near me
And makes me a part of itself
And makes my heart beat
In time with the heart of everything—God.
Simply to be has become a blessing.

In Memory of Hiroshima

On August 6, 1945, the United States dropped a single atomic bomb on Hiroshima. The atomic bomb destroyed 4.7 square miles of the city. More than 92,000 persons were killed. Others died later from the effects of atomic radiation. Three days later, another atomic bomb was dropped on the city of Nagasaki, killing some 40,000 people. Because such utter devastation and brutality toward men, women and children shows the full-blown evil of war, August 6 may be an appropriate time for a family to pause to renew a personal, family pledge for peace.

This service of remembrance is not appropriate for very young children. When children enter an age where they are aware that atrocities have occurred and do occur, care must still be taken not to introduce them to more than they can handle. Remembering past tragedies *must* be accompanied by a firm grip on hope, by a confidence that people who care can make the world a better place in which to live.

For young children, reading a story like *Sadako and the Thousand Paper Cranes*, followed by the St. Francis prayer and song included below, may be an appropriate way to remember.

For older children, the following readings from a "Liturgy to Remember," pulled together by Allan Howe, may be helpful. The Pledge of Nonviolence is probably only appropriate for mature children.

92. Liturgy to Remember

Leader: (*read Micah 4:1–5.*)

Pray together: Lord, make me an instrument of thy peace.
Where there is hatred, let me sow love.
Where there is injury, pardon.
Where there is doubt, faith.
Where there is despair, hope.

Where there is darkness, light.
And where there is sadness, joy.

O Divine Master, grant that I may not so
   much seek to be consoled as to console.
To be understood, as to understand.
To be loved, as to love.

For it is in giving that we receive.
It is in pardoning that we are pardoned.
It is in dying that we are born to eternal life.

—St. Francis of Assisi

Sing together: "Let There Be Peace On Earth" *(See page 124)*

Pray: *(joining hands)* Our Father who art in heaven . . . *(completing the Lord's Prayer)*

Sing together: "Amazing Grace" *(or another familiar song)*

All together—A Pledge of nonviolence: Recognizing the violence in my own heart, yet trusting in the goodness and mercy of God, I pledge for one year to practice the nonviolence of Jesus who taught us in the Sermon on the Mount:

"Blessed are the peacemakers, for they shall be called [the] sons [and daughters] of God . . . You have learned that it was said, 'Love your neighbor and hate your enemy.' But I tell you: 'Love your enemies and pray for those who persecute you, that you may be [daughters and] sons of your [Creator] in heaven.' "

Before God the Creator and the Sanctifying Spirit, I pledge to carry out in my life the love and example of Jesus:

—by striving for peace within myself and seeking to be a peacemaker in my daily life;

—by accepting suffering rather than inflicting it;

—by refusing to retaliate in the face of provocation and violence;

—by persevering in nonviolence of tongue and heart;

—by living conscientiously and simply so that I do not deprive others of the means to live;

—by actively resisting evil and working nonviolently to abolish war and the causes of war from my own heart and from the face of the earth.

God, I trust in your sustaining love and believe that just as you gave me the grace and desire to offer this, so you will also bestow abundant grace to fulfill it. Amen.

Leader: May the peace of the Lord be with you, and with your friends and your neighbors too.

Let it be, let it grow, and everywhere you go, may the peace of the Lord follow you.

Let us offer each other the sign of peace.

Embrace each other saying: May the peace of the Lord be with you.

Let There Be Peace on Earth

Let peace be-gin with me, Let this be the mo-ment now.

With ev-'ry step I take, Let this be my sol-emn vow: To

take each mo-ment and live each mo-ment In peace e-ter-nal-ly.

Let there be peace on earth And let it be-gin with me.

Let it be-gin with me.

Back to School

93. Setting Personal Goals

In order to bring closure to the summer and to prepare for the return to school, the Shufords have a family gathering on one of the last evenings before school starts. Lois bakes a cake for the celebration and writes the names of each of the schools the children will be attending that year on top of the cake with colored icing.

Ahead of time, Bob and Lois choose a scripture verse for each child which seems well suited to speak to what that particular child is dealing with at the time. The verses are written on cards and given to the children as their "watchword" for the new school year.

During the evening meeting, everyone—parents and children—writes out personal goals for the next year. Goals might include: "Do better in math"; "Keep better study hours"; or "Make more friends." The goals are personal and need not be shared with the family, though often they are. Each person seals his or her goals in an envelope. Six months later, the envelopes are opened and everyone checks to see how he or she is doing.

94. Special Breakfast and Prayers

The first day of school in the Vogt home always began with a very special breakfast (which usually included bacon, not normally on the menu!). There were individual prayers for each child. The table was often beautifully set with a Bible verse at each person's place.

Last Day of School

95. Guarding Against After-School Blues

The last day of school is perhaps as deserving of commemoration as the first day. Brigitte Krummel explains that she tried to have new craft materials and new books on hand so that the letdown of the final day wouldn't be so traumatic. Having given some forethought to summer projects, she could help to ease the child from the ordered classroom environment into more personally chosen and directed activities.

96. School's-Out Party

Neta Jackson likes to have a School's-Out Celebration with ice cream and other treats to mark a significant milestone in her child's life. The completion of a whole year of school work deserves to be celebrated with fanfare and fun.

Halloween and All Saints Day

Many families are looking for alternatives to Halloween, a holiday which for many has become excessively horrific and even dangerous. Folks at Reba Place have several suggestions.

97. Making Halloween "Plain Old Fun"

Neta Jackson acknowledges that though for others Halloween has been a negative experience, it has never been so for her family. If everyone dresses up, kids as well as parents, Halloween can be "plain old fun," she asserts. Parents can downplay the ghoulish aspects and emphasize instead the hilarity of disguising oneself and clowning around for an evening. A Halloween party, in which both parents and children participate, can be a frolic for all with bobbing for apples, games, a costume parade and refreshments aplenty.

A prepared bag of goodies for each of the children could replace trick-or-treating, though trick-or-treating can be amusing if parents walk along.

98. Impersonating Saints at an All Saints Party

Halloween comes just a day before All Saints Day. The juxtaposition of the two days allowed an alternative to emerge at Reba Place, that of impersonating saints rather than ghosts and goblins.

Who is a saint? Traditionally, saints are individuals whose personal influence still radiates the best of what human beings can become centuries after they have died. One might call saints "great experimental Christians" who, because of their exceptional self-dedication, made the great discoveries about God that continue to teach us in our day. A saint is a human being who has been transformed by love and inspires us to become better people.

In actuality, all of us who belong to the family of God are saints—chosen and holy (Colossians 3:12–17). But it is appropriate to feature specific outstanding people who inspire and guide us toward godliness. And All Saints Day is an excellent opportunity to do so.

Folks at Reba Place have occasionally had an All Saints Party. A family could as well—perhaps by inviting several other families to participate.

Each person picks a saint and does research on who he or she was and what he or she contributed to our faith heritage. Saints could include Old Testament persons, New Testament persons, persons from church history or contemporary individuals. Each person then dresses as that saint for the party (or at least comes prepared to tell the story of a saint).

Early in the evening, there is a guessing game as one by one the "saints" present themselves and either act out their part or tell a bit about themselves until their identity is guessed.

The evening can also include games and refreshments.

99. A Lantern Walk with "Light" Songs

Another idea for All Saints Day is to go on a Lantern Walk. Everyone in the family, and others from several families, can make simple lanterns (as shown below). The lanterns can be used for a lighted walk through the neighborhood after dark in order to serenade the neighbors with songs using images of light.

1. Find a clean, empty can. Remove paper. Use medium-to-large size.
2. Fill with water and freeze.
3. With hammer and large nail, punch holes in the side to make a design.
4. Make a hole in center of bottom for a nail to hold a candle.
5. Make a hole on either side of rim to string with wire or heavy cord.
6. Soak in hot water to release ice.
7. Dry.
8. Put wide head nail through bottom.
9. Soften bottom of votive candle and press down on nail.
10. With bottle opener, make three triangular slits in side near bottom. Press in halfway.

100. A Song-Lantern Festival

An alternative to the Lantern Walk would be to meet with lanterns in someone's backyard for an outdoor Song-Lantern Festival. A list of "light" songs could be made ahead of time. If the group is large enough, divide in half and sing, facing each other across the backyard, lanterns in hand. Celebrate the light of Christ that dispells darkness, until either voices or songs give out. Then enjoy hot cider and popcorn together.

Succot—Feast of Booths

Succot (soo-kot) is the "feast of booths" celebrated in the fall. It commemorates the dwelling in booths in the wilderness after the Exodus from Egypt (Leviticus 22:33–44). It was, as Sara Ewing describes it, one of the three great occasions for Israel to assemble in the Temple in Jerusalem (Deuteronomy 16:16). On this occasion, Israel was to remember God's protection and provision.

Succot was also called the "festival of ingathering" (Exodus 23:16, 34:22). It was a time to be thankful for the fall harvest.

101. How to Celebrate Succot

1. Build a *succah*. A succah is a simple frame structure, freestanding or three-sided, using a house or garage as one wall. It can easily be constructed with thin wooden slats or branches lashed together. The roof is generally a lattice, covered with branches and partially open to the sky. The succah, or booth, is decorated with branches, fruits and children's pictures.

2. Eat at least one meal or snack in the succah. If possible, serve a fall fruit or vegetable that hasn't been eaten yet, or has been freshly picked from your garden.

3. During the meal in the succah, conduct a short worship service:
   a) Say a blessing over the bread: "Blessed art thou Lord, our

God, Ruler of the universe, who brings forth bread from the earth."

b) Say a benediction for the succah: "Blessed art thou, O Lord our God, Ruler of the universe, who has sanctified us by thy word and commanded us to dwell in the succah. May your divine presence, O God, abide with us. Spread over us your canopy of peace as we recognize our need for your provision and express our thanks for your care. Satisfy those who are hungry and bring the kingdom of heaven to those poor in spirit."

c) After the meal make a *lulav* by binding together branches of palm, myrtle and willow, or other branch varieties you have on hand. The lulay is thought to represent a variety of people. In the final harvest God will "harvest" peoples from all nations.

d) Wave the lulav branches in all directions saying "Hosanna." Sing a song about salvation or the hope of the fulfillment of the kingdom. (The waving of the lulav symbolizes that God is everywhere and that God's kingdom will fill the earth as the waters cover the sea, as stated in Isaiah 11:9.)

4. Gather together a tithe of your fall harvest from the garden or from apple-picking to give to the poor.

Thanksgiving Grace-Notes

Traditionally on Thanksgiving day a family enjoys a sumptuous feast, a symbol of the bounty for which most of us hardly know how to be adequately thankful. But we try.

102. Thanksgiving, Potluck-Style

Kay Holler explains that she and husband Steve have a tradition of Potluck Thanksgivings. Attendance includes any friends, relatives or acquaintances who are able to come. The Hollers try especially to include folks who have no family meal to go to. Among their guests last year were an Afghan refugee family and a Kenyan chemist.

Kay says that for dinner they have the typical Thanksgiving makings, potluck-style, and following the meal, some kind of program. Last year Steve acted out a monologue he'd prepared about William Bradford's reaction to 20th century society. (Bradford was the governor who proclaimed the first Thanksgiving.)

103. Popcorn Kernel Reminders

Neta Jackson describes a small tradition at her family's Thanksgiving table. At the beginning of the meal, a bowl of unpopped popcorn kernels is passed around. Each person takes two kernels. Then, as the bowl is slowly passed again, each replaces the kernels one at a time, mentioning two things for which he or she is thankful. The first thing each person mentions is a general item for which that individual is thankful. The second is something about the person to the left or right for which the speaker is thankful. The kernels of corn serve simply as a tangible connection with the time of the first Thanksgiving, when the Pilgrims learned about corn from the Indians.

104. Newsprint Thanksgiving Memorial

Judy Belser suggests tacking a roll of newsprint on the wall close to the Thanksgiving table, so that as people mill around before and after the meal, they can write little thank-you notes in bright colors for all to see.

105. Thanksgiving Cards

Sara Ewing describes how she traditionally places cards at everyone's Thanksgiving dinner plate. Each card contains a verse that focuses on the poor and needy, verses like Psalms 41:1-3, Proverbs 22:9, Deuteronomy 15:11 and Proverbs 28:27. Sara's intention in using the little notes is not to stifle thankfulness and enjoyment of the meal, but to remind participants that as they have freely received they should also freely give.

Birthday Celebrations

Birthdays afford a time to recognize each person in turn, a time to acknowledge what a precious, wonderful gift of life each child, parent or friend is.

106. A Party Meal and Favorite Stories

In the Vogt home birthdays were often celebrated with a party-like meal. Family members and friends made birthday cards for the birthday person. Conversation at the meal focused on events and developments in that person's life in the past year. Special birthday celebrations of earlier years were recalled. And it was fun to tell the favorite stories again about what the birthday person did or said as a small child. At the end of the birthday meal the Vogts had a prayer for the birthday person, asking God's blessing and protection for the coming year.

107. Serenading in Bed

In the Jackson home birthday celebrations start early. Before the birthday person is out of bed, everyone else carries a lit candle to the honored one's bedside and serenades him or her into the new day and year.

All day the birthday child is excused from chores. He or she can select the menu for a birthday dinner made to order.

108. A Birth Candle and Music

At the birth of each of her daughters, Brigitte Krummel bought a heavy white "birth" candle. Using colored wax or beeswax, Brigitte personalized each candle by adding flowers and a verse which she selected especially for each child. Brigitte wrote the verse in lines around the base of the candle, shaping each letter with rounded strands of soft wax.

At her daughters' births, Brigitte also selected a piece of music—classical or spiritual—for each child. On each succeeding birthday through the years, each child's own birth candle is lit (and stays lit for much of the day), and the music selection is played as the child awakens, at breakfast and perhaps again in the evening. Through the years Brigitte builds the candle up with additional wax so that it never burns down through the personalized, decorative base.

The Krummel family also has the tradition of serenading each birthday person in bed early in the morning with candles, songs and recorders.

109. A Birthday Menu-to-Order and Reminiscences

Bob and Lois Shuford comment on birthdays in their home: "The birthday person, Mom and Dad included, gets to choose whatever he or she wishes for breakfast and dinner meals, within limits of course. As we have dinner, Mom and Dad share something we remember about when we were the age our child is turning (for example, when Gabe turned 8, Dad recalled that when he was 8 he did 12 chin-ups on a chin-up bar in the back yard, and has a picture somewhere to prove it!). If grandparents are with us, they join in too. If it is one of the parent's birthdays, we recall something from when we were the ages of each of our kids."

After the meal, gifts are given one at a time by the person who is actually giving that gift.

In the Shuford small group, the birthday celebration ends with a prayer of blessing, during which all participants gather around to lay hands on the birthday person. The birthday person mentions what he or she looks forward to in the next year. Then one by one, each small-group member asks the Lord's blessing on many different aspects of the birthday person's life.

110. Homemade Cards

Many Reba Place families and small groups have the tradition of making homemade cards for the birthday person. The cards are thoughtful, imaginative and affirming. Often, the individuals around the table who made the cards read aloud any words of love they've written before giving the card. The cumulative effect of several thoughtful cards read aloud is that of a rousing tribute in honor of a much loved person.

111. A Scrapbook, Wreath, and Quilt Patches

Sara Ewing explains that the night before a child's birthday, after he or she has gone to bed, the rest of the family puts up birthday decorations to surprise the child in the morning.

In addition to other traditions already mentioned, the Ewings read from the children's baby books on their birthdays and retell funny things the child used to say, to the merriment of all at the table.

The parents also add a new birthday page every year to each child's scrapbook, with a letter from either parent about highlights from the child's just-completed year.

For the birthday dinner Sara suggests making a wreath of flowers to place on the birthday child's head.

For those with needlework skills, Sara suggests making a quilt patch each year for each child, a "memory square," using themes from the child's favorite drawings, activities or foods. After enough squares have accumulated, they can be fitted together and quilted into a priceless work of beauty and love.

112. Four Questions for the Birthday Person

Lindy Combs remembers four questions which were regulars in her childhood home at the birthday dinner table. Each birthday person knew the questions ahead of time and so came prepared. Everyone pitched in to fill out the picture and liven up the time of fellowship.

Questions:
1. Where and when were you born?
2. What were the most significant events of the past year?
3. What is your hope for the coming year?
4. What are the hopes of others around the table for the birthday person?

113. A Favorite Birthday Song

Marcia Lind says that her family has enjoyed singing "Father, Bless This House," on birthdays and on many other occasions. The lyrics are appropriate for honoring one another on birthdays or graduation, for grandparents when they visit and for anybody special.

Father, Bless this House
(song to someone Special)

Words & Music by Nancy Miner

Fa-ther, bless this house and all with-in. Thank you for the food we share. Thank you for giv-ing Ma-ry to us; (name) Keep her in your ten-der (him) care. Thank you for the joy and for the pain; thank you for the way we grow; Thank you that through each oth-er's lives More and more your love we know.

© 1978 by Reba Place Church. Used by permission.

114. Two Birthday Liturgies

Families may want to use a birthday liturgy before or after the birthday dinner. Larry Clark compiled two liturgies which can serve as rededication services at the beginning of a new year of life. All who participate should come prepared with a verse they have selected to read to the birthday person. A large "Christ candle" is needed, as well as a smaller unlit candle, and for the second service, a stone on which to strike a match.

Birthday Celebration

First Reader: As we gather together to celebrate your birthday, _____ , we want to thank God for giving you to us, and we want to encourage you in fulfilling the purpose for which God created you.

(Light large Christ candle in the center of the table.)

Second Reader: We light a candle to symbolize that Jesus is the source of your life, not only because He made you, but because He constantly gives you spiritual life.

Third Reader: The Bible tells us that you were created with God's personal attention. Psalm 139:13-16 says:

All: For you created my inmost being;
　　you knit me together in my mother's womb.
I praise you because I am fearfully and wonderfully made;
　　your works are wonderful,
I know that full well.
My frame was not hidden from you
　　when I was made in the secret place.
When I was woven together in the depths of the earth,
　　your eyes saw my unformed body.
All the days ordained for me were written in your
　　book before one of them came to be.

Fourth Reader: Psalm 22:9-10 tells us that God watched over you when you were young and helpless:

All: You brought me out of the womb;
　　you made me trust in you

even at my mother's breast.
From birth I was cast upon you;
    from my mother's womb you have been my God.

Fifth Reader: And now we want to give you some nourishment from the scriptures to strengthen your trust in the Lord and your commitment to fulfill the purpose for which He created you.

(Each person reads the verse they have selected for the celebrated one, going around the table. An unlit candle is passed from reader to reader as the verses are read. After all the verses are read, the unlit candle is placed in the hands of the celebrated one. The following is then read:)

Sixth Reader: We ask you, _____ , to light your candle from the Christ candle to signify your willingness to begin another year of life, your thankfulness for God's gift of life through Jesus, and your desire to give all that you have and are to the Loving and Sovereign One for another year.

(Close with a song of dedication.)

Birthday Litany

First Reader: "The people walking in darkness have seen a great light; on those living in the land of the shadow of death a light has dawned."

(A match is struck from a stone on the table and the Christ candle is lit.)

Second Reader: We light the Christ candle from a spark struck from a stone symbolizing the stone rolled from the tomb.

All: Christ has died, Christ is risen, Christ will come again. Hallelujah!

Third Reader: *(alternative for adults)* As we celebrate your physical birth this evening, _____ , we also want to celebrate your spiritual birth. As with Christians of old we present you with a candle to signify your identification with Christ. With the candle we give you some nourishment from the Scriptures.

(alternative for children) _____ , we are glad that God brought you into the world. As we celebrate your

birthday we give you a candle and some verses from the Bible.

(*As the unlighted candle is passed around the table, each person reads a verse they have selected for the celebrated one while holding the candle. As the last one before the birthday person holds the candle, the following is read:*)

Fourth Reader: Jesus said, "While I am in the world, I am the light of the world."

Fifth Reader: Jesus also said, "I have come into the world as a light, so that no one who believes in me should stay in darkness."

(*The person beside the celebrated one lights the candle and hands it to him or her as the following is read:*)

All: As Jesus said to his followers, we say to you, and hope that it will be true in your life. "You are the light of the world, a city that is set on a hill cannot be hid. You were once darkness, but now you are light in the Lord. Walk as a child of the light."

(*Sing a closing "light" song.*)

Yearly Silent Retreat

A tradition which is encouraged at Reba Place is that of a yearly retreat. John and Joanna Lehman describe the how and why of spending several days a year alone with God:

"It is difficult in an active servant life to maintain 'on-target' priorities and good growth patterns. The *urgent* often crowds out the *important*. For this reason we find a yearly retreat of basic importance.

"A retreat is a time to get away from your busy life and all outside distractions long enough to come to a place of inner quiet with the Lord. A retreat is a time to experience God's care for you through listening and meditating on scripture. In the context of experiencing God's great love, you can review the past year and also seek God's direction for making decisions and setting goals for the coming year.

"While on retreat, it is important to have enough time to disengage and become free from inner and outer distractions. A weekend or a three-day retreat is the minimum recommended length. A five-to-eight-day retreat, when it is possible, is more adequate and a great blessing.

"We strongly encourage the experience of some *guided* retreats. You may be fortunate enough to have a retreat house with skilled directors in your area. If not, it would be worth going some distance for such a retreat at least several times in your life. ('The Hermitage' with Gene and Mary Herr as directors, is a Mennonite staffed retreat place at 11321 Dutch Settlement, Three Rivers, Michigan, 49093.) There are Catholic retreat houses in many places with excellent staff who direct ecumenically.

"A retreat on your own can be helpful if you have a clear sense of what you should focus on and resources for guiding meditation. We encourage consulting a pastoral person for suggestions. Such a person can serve as a resource if you get stuck mid-retreat or if you want to share or test insights you have received. If you are not going to a retreat house, it is important to at least be out of your home setting.

"One possibility for a retreat is a friend's home while they are on vacation. If overnight accommodations are unavailable, you could perhaps use a friend's home during the day when they are at work, or you could pack your meals and spend several days in the out-of-doors, or go to a library.

"*Alone With the Alone* by George A. Maloney, SJ (Ave Maria Press, Notre Dame, Indiana), is an eight-day retreat guide for use without a director. Portions of it could be used for a shorter retreat; however, it would lose some of its impact because each days builds on what has gone before."

Chapter Five
Occasional and Life Cycle Rites

A Celebration for Every Occasion

The pace of our lives is often like flipping through a photo album in such haste that the pictures become one meaningless blur. The child beside us pleads, "Mama, slow down. I can't see the pictures." But Mom responds, "There's no time to stop and look. We have to move fast or we won't get through the whole book in time."

Celebration is stopping, looking, embracing and cherishing individual moments in time. All minutes need not look alike. Rather than one unending, tedious rush through time, celebration is stopping the clock in order to enter the Great Time.

Families with a thirst for the eternal and a keen appreciation of their physical environment are well on their way to learning to celebrate anytime, anywhere. It doesn't take an elaborate stage production to bring off a successful family celebration. But it does take a willingness to hallow small moments of meaning. I'm reminded of the spontaneous celebration in Jesus' story of the Prodigal Son. When the wayward young man returned home, his father told the servants, "Quick! Bring the best robe and put it on him. Put a ring on his finger and sandals on his feet. Bring the fattened calf and kill it. Let's have a feast and celebrate. For this son of mine was dead and is alive again; he was lost and is found."

Marking Time For Each Other

With care, and a little forethought, families can help to "mark time" for each other. Rites of passage among obscure jungle tribes have been vividly portrayed on the pages of *National Geographic* magazine. Anthropology texts give graphic descriptions of birthing, puberty and marital rites among exotic native peoples. Our modern ceremonies pale in comparison. We often get away with little more than affixing our signature to a certificate of one kind or another. However, there is little evidence that our secularized world has lessened the need for ritualized expression of an individual's transition from one status to another.

Transitions are often tough times. We know things will be different when we move to a new home or a new family member arrives or a grandparent dies, but we don't know how the changes will affect us. We don't know if we will be able to cope.

Celebrations at times of transition are a way for families to say:

we're in this together; the changes may be tough but we'll link arms to help each other get through; we will stop to take stock of where we've come from and where we are going; we will pause for worship and special prayer because transitions make us feel vulnerable and a little frightened.

Celebrations for Anytime and Anywhere

Once a family has caught the spirit of celebration, no prescribed format is necessary. Every shared experience can become a celebration when Christ is present. This doesn't mean there's no need for planning ahead. Meaningful celebrations are well planned, with ample room for flexibility and spontaneity.

We all do well to remember that it is important to make a celebration fit the family, and not the other way around. Each family must allow its own character to shape an event so that the time together will truly reflect its own unique identity.

Several small, traditional gestures of support at Reba Place, offered to parents of a newborn, serve wonderfully to reassure a family in transition.

A Baby's Birth and Arrival Home

Several small, traditional gestures of support at Reba Place, offered to parents of a newborn, serve wonderfully to reassure a family in transition.

115. A Baby Shower

Baby showers at Reba Place are usually attended by men and women. This has proven significant in reassuring both parents, from the start, that a baby belongs to the whole community and that women and men will join in nurturing the new child. The shower is a social event with games, refreshments and good fellowship, in addition to the gift-giving.

116. A Message of Love

After the baby is born and before the parents arrive home from the hospital (assuming the baby was born in a hospital), friends and family sign messages of love and congratulations on large sheets of paper or newsprint which are then displayed in prominent places in the couple's home.

117. A Week of Effortless Meals

Shortly before the baby's due date, a close friend of the couple coordinates a schedule of volunteers who will bring in a main meal each day for a least a week after the mother and baby arrive home. The prospect of a delightful meal, provided by dear friends every day of that first week of adjustment, provides an enormous boon to the somewhat fragile self-confidence of the parents.

Baby Dedication

Frequently, after a family has recuperated and feels ready to meet the world again, they will present their new baby to the church during a worship service, telling about their thanksgiving for their little one and asking for support as they shoulder the task of parenting.

In a recent child dedication during a regular Sunday morning worship service at Reba Place, Mike and Marianne Lembeck shared about their joy on becoming parents. Excerpts of their presentation are included below to illustrate how parents can personally enter into the dedication of their child to God and to the church.

First, Mike read some thoughts from his journal. Then Marianne said:

"Dear Zoe Beth, I just can't believe you are finally here. Your papa and I have waited a long time for you. You are perfectly made. Who else but the Lord could have done it? He has known and loved you from before the foundation of the world. He knew exactly when you were to be born and who your parents were to be. There are no words to express how deeply grateful to the Lord I am that He has chosen us to care for you.

"Zoe, I know that you belong to the Lord and I pray that I can love you and not hold you so tightly that I can't let you go. The Lord has a plan for your life, to give you a future and a hope. I look forward with joy, fear, some anxiety and excitement to see that plan unfold."

Mike and Marianne together said to their daughter:

"Zoe, you are God's gift of life to us. We love you and want to share with you the best thing we've ever found—life with God through Jesus the Messiah. There is no one like Him. We commit ourselves to raising you in the nurture and fear of the Lord, to so know the love of God that you will be won by it and love Him in return, that you might find fullness of life in Him and be all He created you to be. We also want to raise you to know and love your Jewish heritage.

"Zoe Beth Lembeck, you are a child of the Most High God. You have the best Dad in the whole world. May your life redound to the praise of His glory now and forevermore."

Following the parents' words, the whole church joined in a prayer of dedication for Zoe. Mike then took Zoe from her mother's arms and danced to the strains of an exalting song of praise, holding Zoe high above his head.

118. A Congregational Response

During a child dedication service, parents may desire a formal spoken commitment of support from the church along the lines of the response below. An entire liturgy of scriptures and responsive readings could be prepared by the parents, along with the pastor, for a meaningful, personalized service of dedication.

Parents: We want to teach our children the way of faith in Christ by our example and by our words. We ask for your support and active partnering in our task of parenting. We need your encouragement. We entrust our child to your loving care in this community of faith.

Church: You have asked us to participate in the nurture of your child. We humbly accept our partnering responsibility for sustaining the spiritual, emotional and physical well-being of your child. We offer the gift of ourselves, as representatives of God's large family, to your child. We offer the strength of our common Christian faith. By our example and our words, we will support your calling as parents.

Moving Day

"Moving people from one living space to another can be a surprisingly enjoyable activity at Reba Place Church," writes Anne Gavitt, "which may be one reason we find ourselves doing it so often. There is always work to do, of course, and some of it is hard work, but the strategy of involving as many brothers and sisters as possible makes things quite a bit easier and a lot more fun.

"The people in the human conveyor belt stretching from house door to van are not simply handing boxes to each other. They are meeting each other for the first time or catching up on the news with someone they haven't talked to for awhile. Some may be guests or visitors finding out what the church and community are like. I have occasionally heard 'movers' patiently answering the questions of a neighbor who had stopped by wondering what on earth was going on.

"For me, the only missing ingredient on these occasions was a song. I mentioned this to a friend once, while in a moving line, and he suggested I write one. There was only one possible response and the result follows. It was first performed at a Coffee House evening at Reba Place Church. However, the first time it fulfilled its true purpose was nearly a year later when it entertained a crew who were helping a family move. The following day it was sung upon request during Sunday worship. I called this song 'Make A Line,' but the church seems to have named it 'The Moving Song.' "

The Moving Song

1) It was Saturday morning—I'd just moved in
　　a couple of days before.
When I heard these stomping feet on the stairs;
　　heard the slamming of a door.
Gone was the hope of sleeping in,
　　I didn't want to start the day,
But even with a pillow pulled over my head
　　I could hear some joker say:

Chorus:　Make a line! Make a line!
　　　　　From the skylight to the sidewalk
　　　　　Make a line! Make a line!
　　　　　Don't drop that piano,
　　　　　Take a box and pass it on,
　　　　　Do some work and have some fun.
　　　　　Make a line, make a line, make a line!

2) Well I gave up! I got up and I threw on
　　shirt and jeans.
Stumbled across to open my door;
　　my eyes met quite a scene.
The whole stairwell was full of folks
　　from the foot up to the head,

And a guy with a beard smiled and handed me a box,
   and this is what he said:

Chorus: Make a line! . . .

3) The next I knew I was clear downstairs,
   still handing things along;
 Like chairs and sofas and crates of books;
   I didn't feel too strong.
 My head was spinning as I tried to watch
   the stuff as it passed by.
 An incredible assortment of domestic necessities
   met my wondering eye.

4) There were books and bricks and boards and files,
 Sofa cushions, lamps and piles
 Of magazines; there were rolled-up posters,
 More books, picture frames and coasters,
 A bag of garbage (these folks aren't wasters),
 Fisher-Price airport and marble chasers,
 Teddy bears, dogs and frogs and dolls,
 Sleeping bags, tents, fishing poles;
 Still more books, big potted plants,
 Hangers with dresses, coats and pants,
 Pacifiers, diapers, building blocks,
 Drawers full of underwear and socks,
 And from the garage a collection of bikes,
 Big wheels, carpenter's tools, old trikes,
 Weber Grill, chest freezer that weighed a ton,
 Mysterious projects left undone . . .

(spoken) Well, I'll bet you're wondering how I managed to remember all this stuff. That's because just as I was about to collapse, exhausted on the sidewalk, I was informed that we were halfway through. A short time later, standing outside and looking up at another three-story apartment building, I realized I was going to get the chance to look at it all over again—backwards . . .

5) Those mysterious projects left undone,
   Weber grill, chest freezer that weighed a ton,
   Disappeared somewhere along with the bikes,

Big wheels, carpenter's tools and trikes.
Back came the underwear and socks,
Pacifiers, diapers, building blocks,
Hangers with dresses, coats and pants,
Crates of books, big potted plants,

Sleeping bags, tents, fishing poles,
Teddy bears, dogs and frogs and dolls,
Fisher-Price airport and marble chasers,
The garbage . . . again . . .?
More books, picture frames and posters,
Same old magazines in piles
And the last of the books, bricks, boards and files . . .

(spoken) I tell you, I learned something that day. Never again will I allow simple curiosity to lure me from my bed at the sound of a mysterious voice, no matter what it says. But especially not if it says:

Chorus: Make a line! . . .

The Blessing of Houses

Shortly after a family moves into a new home it is traditional in some circles for a priest to come and ask God's blessing on each room of the home. The ceremony allows a family to dedicate themselves and their home to God. The ceremony is a reminder that all space is sacred space when we ask God to fill it. Really, the house blessing is appropriate at any time a family wants to rededicate their home, perhaps yearly, right after the New Year.

The liturgy below is adapted from "The Blessing of Houses" from the Episcopal Church's lesser liturgies, and from "Prayers at a House Blessing" reported in an Associated Parishes leaflet, both of which have been used at Reba Place.

Various members of the family may want to lead out in the prayers, or the family may want to invite a pastor or significant friends to share in the experience. One could put unlit candles in each room which are lit after each prayer, or an empty vase in each room in which a flower is placed after each prayer. Songs familiar to the family could be inserted throughout.

119. House Blessing Service*

(in Entrance Way)

Leader: *(as all gather at entrance way)* Peace be to this house and to all who enter here.

Family: May the Lord preserve our going out and our coming in, from this time forth and forevermore.

(Pause for silent prayer, candle lighting, flower or song.)

(in the Living Room)

Leader: A new commandment I give to you: Love one another. I have loved you so you must love one another. All people will know that you are my disciples if you love one another (John 13:34,35).

Family: All loving Father, we thank you for our gathering here together. We ask you to bless this meeting place, that it may give to us and to all who come here an opportunity for the full range of human companionship, from the fun of play, through the joys of fellowship, to the divine celebration of your presence in our home.

(Pause for silent prayer, candle lighting, flower or song.)

(in the Kitchen)

Leader: Praise the Lord, O my soul. He waters the mountains from his upper chambers; the earth is satisfied by the fruit of his work. He makes grass grow for the cattle, and plants for man to cultivate—bringing forth food from the earth: wine that gladdens the heart of man, oil to make his face shine, and bread that sustains his heart. Praise the Lord, O my soul (Psalm 104:13-15).

Family: We thank you, all-loving Creator, for the bodies you have given us, and for delicious and nutritious foods with which to nourish them. We ask you to bless this kitchen, that what is prepared here may be a source of health and vigor, and of satisfaction and good cheer, through Jesus Christ our Lord.

(Pause for silent prayer, candle lighting, flower or song.)

(in the Dining Room)

Leader: So do not worry, saying, "What shall we eat?" or "What shall we drink" or "What shall we wear?" For the pagans run after all these things, and your heavenly Father knows that you need them. But seek first his kingdom and his righteousness, and all these things will be given to you as well (Matthew 6:31-33).

Family: We thank you, heavenly Father, that you place the solitary in families and that families are a source of mutual support and a school of love. Bless this table and we who gather regularly at it, that the fellowship of the common meal may knit us ever more closely into one; and we pray that all who from time to time share in our hospitality may also partake in our blessing and joy, through Jesus Christ our Lord.

(Pause for silent prayer, candle lighting, flower or song.)

(at the Office or Study)

Leader: The fear of the Lord is the beginning of knowledge, but fools despise wisdom and discipline. Trust in the Lord with all your heart and lean not on your own understanding; in all your ways acknowledge him, and he will make your paths straight (Proverbs 1:7, 3:5,6).

Family: Lord God, grant us wisdom, for wisdom is more profitable than silver and yields better returns than gold. She is more precious than rubies; nothing we desire can compare with her. Long life is in her right hand; in her left hand are riches and honor. Her ways are pleasant ways, and all her paths are peace. She is a tree of life to those who embrace her; those who lay hold of her will be blessed. Lord, grant us wisdom (Proverbs 3:13-18).

(Pause for silent prayer, candle lighting, flower or song.)

(in the Parents' Bedroom)

Leader: Save us waking, O Lord, and guard us sleeping, that awake we may watch with Christ, and asleep we may rest in peace.

Family: Eternal God, we thank you that, when you created human-kind, you made them male and female and gave them, in marriage, the opportunity to share in intimate love. We pray that those who dwell in this room may give themselves to each other with generosity, reverence and love.

(Pause for silent prayer, candle lighting, flower or song.)

(in other Bedrooms)

Leader: The Lord is my shepherd, I shall lack nothing. He makes me lie down in green pastures, he leads me beside quiet waters, he restores my soul (Psalm 23:1-3a).

Family: May we lie down and sleep in peace, for you alone, O Lord, make us dwell in safety.

(Pause for silent prayer, candle lighting, flower or song.)

(the final House Blessing at a central location)

Leader: The fruit of righteousness will be peace; the effect of righteousness will be quietness and confidence forever. My people will live in peaceful dwelling places, in secure homes, in undisturbed places of rest (Isaiah 32:17,18).

Family: Lord have mercy upon us.

Christ have mercy upon us.

Lord have mercy upon us.

All: O Lord, we humbly ask you to fill this house with your love and joy and peace. Let your abundant grace and blessing be upon us who make our home herein, that dwelling together in this house made with hands, we may ourselves be evermore your dwelling place, through Jesus Christ our Lord. Thanks be to God! Amen.

(Pause. Light final candle or place final flowers in vase. Sing song of benediction.)

*See note on page 32 about use of inclusive language.

120. Naming Your Home

Folks at Reba Place have traditionally chosen a name for their homes: The Branch, The Clearing, Canaan House, L'Hayim. . . . As part of the house blessing service, a family may want to choose a house name, a name which will express, in brief, the family's affectionate regard and desire for their house.

Open House

Open House is a tradition at Reba Place when a family moves into a new home and wants friends and neighbors to visit, or any time a family wants to get better acquainted with neighbors.

The family sends out notices or invitations to all who would like to stop in for fellowship and refreshments. The evening is informal with folks coming and going, chatting in small groups, and touring the house during a two- to three-hour period.

An Open House is also a nice way to share a special guest with others. If some well-known person, who would be of interest to many in the congregation, is coming to visit, an Open House or informal drop-in is an excellent way to share him or her with the larger church community.

Potpourri Traditions

121. A Party for the Garbage Man

Peggy Belser and several friends have occasionally thrown a party for their regular garbage crew as a gesture of appreciation for the important work the men do in keeping the neighborhood clean. In the morning, when Peggy hears the familiar sounds of the garbage truck, she has been known to run out and invite the men in for a hasty but pleasant treat of rolls with ham and cheese, cranberry juice served in goblets, brownies, and fellowship with friends who appreciate their good work.

122. A Backyard Tradition

In the Vogt home the backyard was a tradition in itself, which got better and better over the years. At its peak, the backyard was a place of beautiful plants and flowers of many domestic and wild varieties.

123. Berry-Picking as a Family Tradition

The Vogt family used to have a blueberry- and strawberry-picking tradition (before the children grew up and left home). These were real adventures, they say, carefully planned at the right time of every summer. The family travelled, as they describe it, to "gorgeous, unbelievable blueberry or strawberry farms where the fruits grew bigger than you could ever remember seeing them before, and the taste was even more unbelievable. Of course, untold hundreds (of berries, that is) never made it into the pickers' pails, going instead to fuel the energies of hard-working pickers! Towards noon, tired, happy, but not-wanting-to-ever-taste-another-berry pickers would head toward home.

"In the fall, it was applesauce time . . . in the spring a trip to Woodstock for rhubarb."

124. A Song on Spotting the First Star

Joanna Lehman remarks that the Lehman family has enjoyed frequent camping excursions. It became an evening tradition over the years of vacationing out under the stars to sing "Evening Star Up Yonder" upon spotting the first star.

Evening Star Up Yonder

1. Ev-ening-star-up-yonder, Teach me like you to Wander. Willing and o-be-dient-ly

the path that God or-dains for me. Evening star up yon-der.

2. Teach me, gentle flowers,
   to wait for springtime showers.
   Through this wintry world to grow
   green and strong beneath the snow;
   Teach me, gentle flowers.

3. Shady lanes refreshing,
   teach me to be a blessing
   To some weary soul each day,
   friend or foe who pass my way;
   Shady lanes refreshing.

4. Mighty ocean teach me,
   to do the task that needs me
   And reflect as days depart
   heaven's peace within my heart;
   Mighty ocean teach me.

5. Evening sun descending,
   teach me when life is ending.
   Life shall pass, and I like you
   shall rise again where life is new:
   Evening sun descending.

The Soda-Pop Routine for a Sick Child

Whenever someone was sick in the Vogt home, a few family traditions came into play. One was pop—soda pop! The one thing every sick child needs, they observe, is plenty of pop. Actually, this means the one thing every sick child needs is a little extra Tender Loving Care. The Vogts relate that they regularly prayed for the sick and, thankfully, the sick regularly recovered.

125. A Sick-Kid-Box

The Shufords suggest preparing a Sick-Kid-Box, filled with toys, crayons, paints and other surprises, that is brought out only on the occasion of a child's illness, and, of course, put away when he or she recovers.

Recognition of Twelve-Year-Olds

Folks at Reba Place and elsewhere have come to understand the twelfth birthday of a child as a critical milestone in a child's maturation. The twelfth birthday has been chosen for several reasons: it was at twelve years of age that Jesus remained behind in the temple courts, after his parents had departed, to interact with the teachers of the law on theological questions. The twelfth birthday affords an opportune time, at the onset of adolescence, to recognize formally that a child is growing up, leaving childish ways behind and embarking on the road to adulthood. Adolescence is frequently a time of great confusion for parents and children, as each adjusts to new ways of relating. A specific rite of passage at the twelve-year marker can provide a significant opportunity to talk about the changes that are in store and to shore up the family resolve to weather them arm in arm.

126. Presenting a Bible

One tradition among Reba Place families is to present a Bible to each child when he or she turns twelve. It is done in the presence of the gathered church, usually on a Sunday morning. (The child may have helped to select the Bible ahead of time.) Mother and Dad each say some affirmative words along the lines of, "Child, it's been a pleasure to have you in our family. We've enjoyed watching you grow in various ways. . . . You are now entering a stage of life where you will want to examine the faith that we taught you and, we trust, make it your own. This Bible, we believe, can be a lamp for your feet and a light on your path. If you will study it, asking the Holy Spirit to teach you, it will become an inspiration for great good in your life. . . ."

The parents have often underlined several outstanding verses which they point out to the child. A special prayer for the child follows with the pastor or close friends often joining in. The child selects a song ahead of time, which the congregation or special music group sings.

The parents and child may also invite important friends to a festive birthday party later at home.

127. A Retreat Weekend for Just Parent and Child

Another emerging tradition at Reba Place, which Lois and Bob Shuford describe, is that of spending a retreat weekend with each child as he or she enters adolescence. The idea is for a parent and child (father-son, mother-daughter) to go away for a weekend together. Bob and his twelve-year-old son recently spent a weekend at a rented cabin in a woods. They cooked their own meals, hiked, listened to a series of tapes on preparing for adolescence and talked a lot. The weekend was a very significant time for father and son to interact on issues that the son, in particular, would be facing. The groundwork for good communication throughout the rocky, peer-pressured adolescent years was strengthened on that weekend together.

Entering Adulthood

When their daughter, Becky, turned thirteen, Lois and Bob took her out for a fancy dinner and have done so every year following— just the parents and daughter. When Becky turns eighteen this year, Bob and Lois each intend to write her a letter, affirming her and releasing her into adulthood. They feel the need to be deliberate about acknowledging that the responsibilities and freedoms of adulthood are now hers to exercise. As parents, they will continue to be available as a resource when she wants their advice, but not as controllers or disciplinarians.

Baptism and First Communion

Mennonites and Brethren practice adult, rather than infant, baptism. When Brigitte Krummel's daughter, Sabine, was baptized, Brigette and her daughter planned the service together, selecting the songs and persons who would be involved. Sabine's friends surprised her with a celebrative dance following the baptism.

Friends and family met in the Krummel home later in the afternoon for Sabine's first communion. The service, led by a family friend, was filled with scripture readings and songs. Different persons who had been asked to share focused on what their first communion had meant to them. Brigitte talked about how she had earlier visualized her daughter as seated in front of her but that now Sabine had moved to sit *beside* her, within the circle of the gathering church. Now mother and daughter were fellow believers, each personally responsible to God for herself.

Graduation Festivities

128. An Armful of Flowers, a Houseful of Friends

When Brigitte's daughter graduated from high school, friends and family members all presented her with flowers so that, at the finale of the celebrative event, her arms were filled with flowers.

Brigitte reserved a table at a restaurant so that close family and friends could move right from the graduation ceremonies to a festive dinner together. Vases had been prepared ahead of time to hold the many flowers.

A weekend after the graduation Brigitte invited friends over for a home-gathering—adults and peers who had been important to her daughter at some point during her growing-up years. The gathering included songs, good fellowship and refreshments. But most significantly, the meeting included a formal time when folks could tell the graduate what she had meant to *them* along the way. Ahead of time, Brigitte had prepared a lengthy statement which she also shared during the gathering. In it she talked about her daughter's growing-up years. Brigitte made a point of telling her daughter how she, as a mother, had learned so much from her child and how she had changed and grown up with and through her daughter.

129. A Scrapbook from Friends

The Shuford family also hosted a gathering of friends on the event of their daughter's graduation. Ahead of time they circulated blank pages of a small scrapbook and asked friends to each fill a page with anything they chose—reminiscences, advice, pictures or poetry. The pages were collected and presented as a surprise gift at the graduation party.

Separations and Farewells

There are many reasons why separations occur within a family or community context: children leaving for college, change of job or church, death in the family. . . . Saying farewell to friends or family is often very hard. The pain which separations evoke makes us want to avoid the whole process altogether. We stuff down our feelings and may leave without even saying good-bye.

Unprocessed separations from significant persons, however, can cause drawn-out, nagging uneasiness, guilt and mistrust, especially in children. For our health and growth, it is important to work through the pain and negative emotions associated with separations so that we can move confidently into new relationships. Folks at Reba Place have used a variety of ways to ease the pain of good-byes.

130. Ideas for Easing a Departure

1) As the departure time of a loved one approaches, plan a festive event in honor of the person who is leaving: a picnic, an evening fireside chat, a fancy meal with flowers and formal table settings.

2) Have everyone write a letter or make a card to give to the person or persons who are leaving, including small children. If thoughtfully prepared, the words of love and acknowledged loss can help to ease the pain of separating and serve as a reminder,

years later, of a cherished relationship.

3) A simple note to a child, which affirms the child and recounts delightful memories, or a small gift for the youngster gives him or her something to hold onto and enjoy again later when loneliness sets in.

4) The evening together can include reminiscing with slides, storytelling and songs. The one who is leaving may want to talk about how he or she feels about saying good-bye, about the meaning of the relationships he or she is leaving behind and about the anticipated changes just ahead.

5) The evening could conclude with communion and prayer.

131. A Memory Book

To capture some of the goodness of having been together, prepare a memory book for the person leaving. Have all participants fill a page of a scrapbook with memories and well wishes. It is hard to imagine a more meaningful parting gift.

132. Hosting an Open House

To simplify the process of getting around to say all the necessary good-byes, host an open house for the person who is leaving. Invite all family and friends, who want to say one last fond farewell, to drop in. Gifts and cards on such an occasion provide one last rush of goodwill which the one departing will remember for a long. time.

Forgiveness and Healing

Forgiveness is the grace that enables bumbling, failing human beings to live together in peace. Ample reasons abound to hold grudges against many people, be they family, acquaintances or governments. Whether we harbor resentment against our parents for having mistreated us, or against our children for spurning our love, or against anyone for doing us wrong, we will sooner or later find ourselves knotted up with debilitating anger. The ability to forgive others is the foundational act of new beginnings and of familial harmony.

133. Untangling a Domestic Snarl

An event occurred in the Shenk home one morning that I share now because I think it illustrates what happens, in one way or another, in any family that knows about forgiveness and new beginnings. It may serve as a helpful "tradition" when there seems to be no other way out of a tense situation.

It was Sunday morning. Dad was out of town. I asked three-year-old Timothy what he would like for breakfast. Timothy said he didn't know, and from all appearances, didn't care. I checked with Joseph. Joseph quickly chose hot oatmeal. I took Timothy's silence to mean acquiescence, so I made a pot of oatmeal, served each of the boys several dollops and sat down with my coffee and sweet roll. At this point, when we were all seated at the table, Timothy declared that he wanted cinnamon toast.

Breakfast was already underway. The oatmeal was served. I didn't feel like jumping up to do more preparations, so I said, "No. It's too late." Whereupon, Timothy threw a scene, crying and heatedly objecting.

On the heels of such an outcry, I couldn't in good conscience give in and say, "Oh well. Cinnamon toast isn't such a big deal. I'll jump up once more and get it." I knew there was no going back. So I explained patiently, "Timothy, you had your chance and now it is time to eat oatmeal. You like oatmeal too, with milk, raisins and brown sugar."

Timothy fussed on, unrelenting. His wails made any mercy on my part impossible lest I reinforce his unacceptable behavior. I'd backed myself into a corner. Neither one of us was going to change our minds. It looked as though we were at an impasse.

I took Timothy on my lap and asked him to stop crying or go to the bedroom. He did stop crying but kept loudly insisting that he wanted toast and only toast! I explained again (less patiently this time) how I had asked him *first* what he wanted and since he hadn't had a preference I'd proceeded with other breakfast preparations. He had missed his chance.

Timothy sat quietly in thought for a moment and then suddenly he looked at me. "Let's start all over!" he said.

Immediately I saw a way out. I laughed. Big brother Joseph, who had watched his mother's intransigence with growing concern, laughed. A big smile spread over Timothy's face.

"Okay," I said, taking a deep breath. "Timothy, what would you like for breakfast?"

His hearty voice rang out. "Cinnamon toast!" He jumped off my lap and happily climbed onto his chair to await its arrival.

134. A Burning Ceremony

Several folks at Reba Place have long given themselves to a healing ministry, working with people who for one reason or another have found it difficult to forgive and experience healing of old wounds. One of the climactic events toward the end of a counseling experience involving the healing of memories, is a Burning Ceremony. John Lehman, a family counselor, related that one dimension of forgiveness and eventual reconciliation is an ability to let go of old resentments.

John asks a person to write down all the ugly, angry feeling he or she has toward others, and to write down any feeling he or she wants to give up to the Lord. John reads several scriptures including I John 1:9 and Hebrews 12:28,29. The paper of written resentments is then tossed into the fire and vividly consumed.

Prayer for forgiveness and release follows, with a concluding song of celebration. (If no fireplace is available, the paper can be lit with a match and thrown into a large kettle.)

One could use a Burning Ceremony within a family context for a variety of reasons. One might be to eliminate certain common but unhelpful household words: for example, when the children complain a lot saying, "It's not fair, it's not fair!" If Mom and Dad try hard to keep things fair and don't appreciate the accusations, they could have everyone sit down, discuss why the words are unhelpful, write out the words to be eliminated on pieces of paper, agree not to use them anymore and toss them into the fire. Such a ceremony can serve to seal a family pact that certain frequent complaining or coarse words are not acceptable family parlance.

A Burning Ceremony could also be used if there are widespread regrets about a particular family argument. A family meeting could be called where individuals write down any leftover feelings related to the incident and burn them. The burning could be followed by embraces and prayers. (A precaution: such events must be handled with enormous sensitivity. They can't be contrived or forced but must reflect a willingness and desire for reconciliation on the part of the participants.)

135. A Litany of Healing*

A Litany of Healing has been used, on occasion, in Reba Place homes. The one below has been adapted from an unknown source. It could be used in part or in whole for a family or small group gathering focused on prayer for healing. Short sections have been highlighted in bold type for use with young children.

Leader: O God the Father, who desires health and salvation for all people;
All: Have mercy upon us.
Leader: O God the Son, who came that we might have life and might have it more abundantly;

All: Have mercy upon us.

Leader: O God the Holy Spirit, who makes our bodies the temple of your presence;

All: Have mercy upon us.

Leader: O Holy Trinity in whom we live and move and have our being;

All: Have mercy upon us.

Leader: O Son of David, who went about doing good and healed all who came in faith and repentance;

All: Have mercy upon us.

Leader: O Son of David, who sent forth disciples both to preach the Gospel and to heal the sick;

All: Have mercy upon us.

Leader: O Son of David, who pardons all our sins and heals all our infirmities;

All: Have mercy upon us.

Leader: O Son of David, who renews our minds by your spirit who dwells in us;

All: Have mercy upon us.

Leader: O Son of David, whose holy Name is a medicine of healing and a pledge of eternal salvation;

All: Have mercy upon us.

Leader: We call on you to hear us, O Lord, and that you will grant grace to all who are sick, that they may be made whole;

All: We call on you to hear us, O God.

Leader: That you will grant to all who are disabled by injury or sickness, patience, courage and sure faith in you;

All: We call on you to hear us, O God.

Leader: That you will give to all sick children relief from pain, speedy healing and fearless confidence in you;

All: We call on you to hear us, O God.

Leader: That you will grant to all about to undergo an operation your strength, that they will not be afraid;

All: We call on you to hear us, O God.

Leader: That you will grant to all sufferers the refreshment of quiet sleep, that they may rest in you;

All: We call on you to hear us, O God.

Leader: That you will give to all who are lonely or despondent, having no one to comfort them, the sense of your presence;

All: We call on you to hear us, O God.

(Continued)

Leader: That you will restore all who are in mental darkness to soundness of mind and cheerfulness of spirit;

All: We call on you to hear us, O God.

Leader: That you will give to all doctors and nurses your wisdom, that with knowledge, skill and patience they may minister to the sick;

All: We call on you to hear us, O God.

Leader: That you will give to all who search for the causes of sickness and disease the guidance of thy Holy Spirit;

All: We call on you to hear us, O God.

Leader: That you will grant to the servants of your Church such grace, that what is done by their ministry may be perfected by your power.

All: We call on you to hear us, O God.

Leader: Jesus of Nazareth;

All: Have mercy upon us.

Leader: Jesus of Nazareth;

All: Have mercy upon us.

Leader: Jesus of Nazareth;

All: Grant us your peace.

Leader: You are a God who does wonders;

All: You have declared your power among the people.

Leader: For with you is the well of life;

All: And in your light shall we see light.

Leader: Turn to us, O Lord God of hosts;

All: Show the light of your countenance and we shall be whole.

Leader: We wait for your loving-kindness, O God;

All: In the midst of your temple.

Leader: The Lord be with you;

All: And with your spirit.

Leader: Let us pray.

Almighty God, the giver of life and health, who sent your only-begotten Son into the world that all your children might be made whole, send your blessing on all who are sick and upon those who minister to them of your healing gifts, that being restored to health of body and of mind, they may give thanks unto you, through Jesus Christ our Lord. Amen.

See note on page 32 about use of inclusive language.

136. A Family Prayer for Healing

When illness occurs in a family, Virgil Vogt suggests that a family prayer for healing become a regular part of family life. When a child or parent is ill, a simple bedside prayer focuses minds and hearts on the One who has promised to be with us always.

Preserving Family Memories

137. Grandma's Scrapbook

The Shuford grandmother has the delightful practice of saving everything she receives from each child—letters, Christmas lists, pictures, etc. She has a scrapbook for each child, to which she continually adds things as she gets them. Grandchildren have been known to spend hours of enjoyment paging through their own partially filled scrapbook when they visit Grandma. Grandmother's plan is to finally give each child his or her scrapbook at college graduation or wedding time.

138. A Book of Letters and a Family Diary

Neta Jackson is making a book for each of her children. In it she has written letters to each child about his or her birth. Through the years she and Dave have written other letters to the children. The letters aren't for the children to read immediately. They serve, rather, to capture some of the parental feelings and concerns as the child grows. Neta and Dave will give the books to the children when each marries or finally leaves home.

Neta also keeps a Family Diary. To help her in the process, everyday she records on a block calendar just a few words about the day's events. Then every three months or so, Neta takes the time to look over the calendar and gather together the events for recording in a hardcover book with blank pages.

139. A Scrapbook at High School Graduation

Joanna Lehman prepared a scrapbook for each of her children on the event of their high school graduation, using photos, artwork and cards collected over the years. She remarked that working on such a scrapbook can help in the parental grieving process as parents begin gradually to deal with the child's expected leaving.

140. A Family Celebrations Book as a Wedding Gift

Virgil and Joan Vogt prepared a "Family Celebrations" book as a wedding gift for their daughter. The focus of the book was on cherished family traditions that their daughter might want to carry on in her own new home. The book includes pictures, descriptions and poetry. A more significant and delightful wedding gift would be hard to come by.

Praying for Peace

A family peace service could include the reading of several scriptures and a litany, like the one below from the Episcopal Peace Fellowship, contributed by Linas Brown. Parents could shorten and simplify the litany for use with younger children (see highlighted sections set in bold type).

The lovely Hebrew melody below is likely to become a favorite family benediction for many comings and goings.

Scripture readings: Colossians 3:12-15
John 14:23-29

141. A Litany of Intercession for Peace

Leader: For the citizens of all countries, that they act not as enemies or aliens, but welcome each other as brothers and sisters, let us pray to the Lord.

All: Lord, God of peace, hear our prayer.

Leader: For our brothers and sisters who are victims of the abuse of wealth and power, that they be speedily restored to their human dignity, let us pray to the Lord.

All: Lord, God of peace, hear our prayer.

Leader: That all men and women everywhere may find just and profitable employment and the fulfillment of their vocation, both human and divine, let us pray to the Lord.

All: Lord, God of peace, hear our prayer.

Leader: For all government and military officials, church leaders and business leaders, that they may make effective the rule of justice and right, let us pray to the Lord.

All: Lord, God of peace, hear our prayer.

Leader: Lord, help us to build bridges rather than fences and to choose struggle rather than compliance to discern what we really need security for and defense against.

All: Lord, God of peace, hear our prayer.

Leader: Lord, give us the courage to think out the horrors of nuclear war, to enable us to acknowledge that it can happen here.

All: Lord, God of peace, hear our prayer.

Leader: Lord, help more of us to be peacemakers rather than

peacekeepers, to rely on you more than on ourselves and others.

All: Lord, God of peace, hear our prayer.

All: Lord, we have confidence in your care and concern, and we ask you to bless peacemakers even as the world favors and blesses warriors. Help us to be strong, Lord. We want the country to be strong, strong enough to love you above all, to depend and trust in you above all. We want to be number one, Lord, but not in the capacity to destroy; number one in the capacity to love, to heal and to reconcile. We want to be powerful, Lord, not to threaten the world with destruction, but to show forth the power of your love and concern. We want to be ready and alert, Lord, ready for you when you come in glory. Help us to be channels of your peace. We look to you for life and peace. Amen.

(Give each other the kiss of peace.)

142. A Hebrew Song of Benediction

Peace Be Unto You

Hebrew Melody

Peace be un-to you from the watch-ing an-gels, ye watch-ing an-gels from on high.

Bless us with peace you watch-ing an-gels who bring peace, ye watch-ing an-gels from on high.

Peace from the King, the Ru-ler o-ver all things, the Ho-ly One, bless-ed be He!

Peace from the King, the Ru-ler o-ver all things, the Ho-ly One, bless-ed be He!

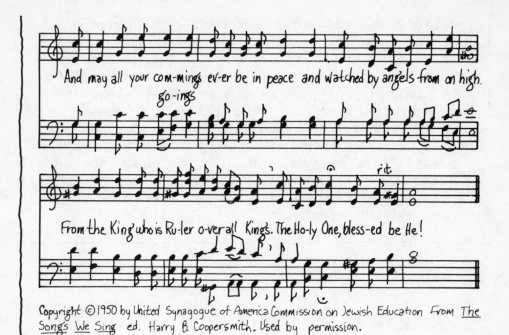

And may all your com-mings ev-er be in peace and watched by angels from on high.
go-ings

From the King who is Ru-ler o-ver all Kings. The Ho-ly One, bless-ed be He!

Copyright © 1950 by United Synagogue of America Commission on Jewish Education. From *The Songs We Sing* ed. Harry B. Coopersmith. Used by permission.

Wedding Plans

Weddings at Reba Place are church-wide affairs, starting with the wedding shower. Since any one family couldn't be expected to reproduce what a cohesive church community can do, I'll make several observations, based on practices at Reba Place, which a family may want to consider while making wedding plans.

143. Alternative Wedding Shower

The couple prepares a gift list of needed items so that gift-giving can be coordinated. Most gifts are given at the wedding shower instead of at the wedding itself. Substantial gifts are often given by the church "small groups" instead of by individuals.

The wedding shower gifts are brought to a "gift receiver" a day or so ahead of time. Only a few close friends and family gather with the couple as they open the gifts, an hour or so before the larger shower gathering. The gifts are put on display for all who come to the shower. The actual shower, then, instead of focusing on the gifts, is a festive time of humorous skits and songs written and selected in the couple's honor. Frequently, original and funny words about the couple are sung to familiar tunes. Often there is opportunity for stories about the couple and words of advice. The evening ends with refreshments.

144. Getting the Community Involved

For the wedding itself, almost everyone in the church gets involved in some way. Tasks are assigned to those who can either prepare the meeting room, arrange flowers, prepare the rehearsal-night dinner, make and decorate the cake, create a new wedding dance, clean up afterwards or take part in the wedding program with words and song. Mobilization of creativity and service on such a large scale is possible in part because there are a few folks willing to be responsible to coordinate tasks and many folks willing to pitch in with doing what they can to make the wedding a community affair.

145. A Wedding Quilt

Several months before the wedding, empty, light-colored quilt squares are distributed (by someone with quilt know-how, obviously) to friends who would like to embroider or applique a design for the wedding couple. The couple indicates only which colors should be dominant throughout. The content of each patch is up to each creator. All patches are to be returned by a set date. They are then assembled, sewn together with a solid colored border and sent off to be quilted. The wedding quilt usually forms a colorful backdrop at the wedding itself.

146. Seven Jewish Blessings

A traditional Jewish bridal canopy has been used in several weddings, as well as an adaptation of the traditional "Seven Blessings":

1. Blessed art Thou, O Lord our God, King of the universe, who has created all things to Thy Glory.

2. Blessed art Thou, O Lord our God, King of the universe, creator of humankind.

3. Blessed art Thou, O Lord our God, King of the universe, who has made man and woman in Thine image, after Thy likeness. Blessed art Thou, O Lord, creator of man and woman.

4. Blessed art Thou, O Lord our God, King of the universe, who has given marriage as the setting in which we may live and grow, experiencing covenant love, steadfastness of purpose and fulfillment of our destiny upon the earth.

5. May she who was barren be exceedingly glad and exult when her children are gathered to her in joy. Blessed art Thou, O Lord, who makest Zion joyful through her children.

6. O make these loved companions greatly to rejoice, even as of old Thou didst gladden Thy creatures in the Garden of Eden. Blessed art Thou, O Lord, who makest bridegroom and bride to rejoice.

7. Blessed art Thou, O Lord our God, King of the universe, who has created joy and gladness, bridegroom and bride, mirth and exultation, pleasure and delight, love, peace and fellowship. O Lord our God, may there continue to be heard in the streets of our cities the voice of joy and gladness, the voice of the bridegroom and the voice of the bride, the jubilant voices of youths from their feast of song. Blessed art Thou, O Lord, who makest bridegroom to rejoice with the bride.

Funerals and Dealing with Grief

Contemporary funeral preparations and all the trappings have become the near exclusive province of funeral directors. Whether because of inexperience or fear, most of us are rendered helpless in the event of a loved one's death. We're only too glad to deliver the body into the hands of experienced professionals, even though they are strangers. We would rather lay out a lot of money for all the "appropriate trappings" than do the funeral preparation ourselves.

Folks at Reba Place have taken measures to reclaim some of the responsibility and privilege of caring for a loved one from the death bed to the grave. Their experience may give some helpful pointers to others who want to enter more actively into this momentous rite of passage.

147. Simplifying and Personalizing Funeral Arrangements

1. Discuss with the funeral director ahead of time, if possible, what is required by law for caring for and embalming a body. Negotiate an arrangement with the director that will allow you to do as much of the preparation as you care to.

2. Make the casket out of pine boards, which are then varnished. (Having a carpenter in the family is definitely an asset.)

3. Work together as family and friends, all night if need be, to make the casket, cover the mattress, sew and gather the lining. The time of lovingly readying the casket can be very therapeutic. It is a marvelous opportunity for beginning to process the death together.

4. Have someone provide food to the workers.

5. Take the readied casket to the funeral home (if embalming was done) to receive the body. Transport it yourself to the meeting-house for the wake and funeral, instead of using a hearse.

6. The evening before the funeral, gather for the wake. Use this time for reminiscing about your loved one, talking to each other, grieving together and celebrating his or her life.

7. After the funeral, transport the casket yourself to the burial ground.

148. One Man's Thoughts on Coping with Grief

Jim Stringham, M.D., whose wife, Charlotte, died in 1985, has since written some thoughts on how to deal constructively with grief. With his permission, here are excerpts from his suggestions.

"These are some of the things I have heard the Lord saying to me as I have been grieving Charlotte's sudden death after 56 years of marriage:

"1. Make a list of all of the things you and Charlotte did (the nitty-gritty everyday pleasures, events and difficulties) that never will be possible again because she died. Take time to do this. Then, in prayer, turn them all over to the Lord. Ask that He will use the Holy Spirit to alert you the instant you start wishing for, getting sad about, pitying yourself or regretting her absence.

"2. Make another list of the things that you will continue to do, things that are necessary for your ongoing life from now on.

"3. Write down your memories. You have loads of happy as well as painful memories. It is all right to think about them and even cry as you think about them. Thank the Lord for those experiences. You need to differentiate these from the first list above. For instance, if you are visiting one of your children again and start thinking, 'I wish Charlotte were here now,' that is nixed out; it is on list No. 1. But you can say, 'I am surely glad we were here last year and Charlotte could see your new home and all the rest.' That is fine.

"4. When you start to think about ways it was hard for Charlotte because of the way you were, the way you did things and so forth, remember there were similar things from Charlotte's side that made it difficult for you. Put them on the scales. They will balance each other. Forget it!

"5. Various people have asked for some of Charlotte's things. You will see them wearing items of clothing that belonged to her. When you see them, let that be an occasion to thank the Lord for the memories you have of her wearing those things, and rejoice.

"6. You repeatedly told Charlotte that if she died first you hoped you could rejoice that she was at last in heaven and free from suffering and pain. She has longed to be there. Rejoice in that fact. Sometimes you will find yourself thinking, 'I wonder what Charlotte is doing now!' Thank the Lord she is with Him, and that eventually you'll see each other again.

"7. A regular daily devotional and a special period of listening to the Lord have been part of your life for years. You will find as you continue to do this, the Spirit will give you many things which help. The prayers of many people praying for you help too.

"8. Birthdays and holidays are usually low points for the bereaved. Take such occasions to recall the many happy times you had together at special celebrations. Make them a time of rejoicing.

"9. Other folks often feel a little awkward when they see you, because they're afraid that talking about Charlotte is a taboo subject. Talk about Charlotte yourself, not only her death, but also things she did and said. By your own freedom you will communicate to others that it is all right to talk about her, that in fact you want to talk about her.

"10. During the last hours while waiting in the intensive care unit, I had written, 'What is going on in my mind? We have prayed for years to die with our boots on. We have affirmed that Jesus will keep Charlotte alive as long as He has anything for her to do. If she dies now, it is the way the Lord has answered that prayer. It will be difficult to adjust, but death is part of life. What God has to tell me about all this is to trust Him and know He will sustain me.' "

Celebrating with Handicapped Persons

Jean Vanier has said, "The poorer people are, the more they love to celebrate." Vanier, who has founded a network of communities for the handicapped all over the world, discusses celebration at length in his book *Community and Growth.*

Celebration helps people to accept the sufferings of everyday life by offering them the chance to relax and let go, he says. The irritations of daily life are swept away when we celebrate. Celebration becomes a sign of resurrection which gives individuals and communities the strength to carry the cross of each day.

Vanier's experience with celebrations that include large numbers of mentally and physically handicapped persons led him to observe:

"I wonder if all joy doesn't spring from suffering and sacrifice. Can those who live in comfort and security, with all they need, really be joyful? I wonder. But I am sure that poor people can be joyful. At times of celebration, they seem to overcome all their suffering and frustration in an explosion of joy. They shed the burden of daily life and they live a moment of freedom in which their hearts simply bound with joy."

How the Sonshine Group Does It

Dale and Martha Cooper minister to a group of handicapped persons called the Sonshine Group at Reba Place. From their extensive experience in festive gatherings with handicapped persons they observe:

"The handicapped have much to teach us about celebration. They, above all, celebrate with their hearts rather than with their intellects. They are often wonderful with the use of their imaginations, uncovering simple joys and pleasures which often go unnoticed by the rest of us. Like the poor, they bring us closer to God because of their weakness and simplicity.

"The handicapped are warm, loving and often very free. They are not bound as much by, 'What will others think of me.' In an atmosphere of trust, they readily give themselves to one another,

179

bonding together as a group.

"Such has been our experience in Sonshine Group. We have wonderful celebrations, lifting up the important moments of our lives in some special way. We have a good time laughing, sharing, praying and sometimes crying together.

149. Birthdays

"Birthdays are an important celebration for us. The birthday person gets to choose the menu. We decorate the table and the chair of the birthday person with brightly colored streamers. During the meal we often celebrate with exploding party favors, noise-makers, and all kinds of balloons. Sometimes we do silly things with the streamers from the party favors, draping them over our hair like spaghetti.

"After our meal and dessert we have a time of sharing around the table about the person. Each group member lifts up at least one positive quality that he or she likes about the celebrated one. After that we have a time of prayer together in which several people pray and ask for God's favor and blessing to be upon the birthday person.

150. Weekly Meal Together

"Our weekly meal on Friday evening is an important celebration for us. After we have prayed and the food has been served around the table, we start our sharing. Each person, in turn, is asked to share about how the week has been. The rest of us listen. The leader of the table and others respond with affirmation and encouragement.

Set-Up and Clean-Up

"An important part of our weekly meal is the set-up and clean-up. Most Sonshine people come early and help set up tables, put out chairs, spread the tablecloths, put on the silverware, get the coffee pot ready, pick up the food and many other tasks. Likewise, after the meal, everyone takes part in cleaning up, doing the dishes, vacuuming, taking down tables, etc. We have found a great deal of joy in working together. We often joke around and have a good time as we work. This really helps everyone to feel owner- ship in the group. Everyone is able to contribute in some way. Everyone is important.

151. Prayer Time

"Our prayer times, after the weekly meal and clean-up, are im- portant times when we bond our hearts to Jesus and to one an- other. We lift up Jesus as the center in all of our celebrations. In prayer we are learning to celebrate the love of Jesus both through the spoken word and through the beauty of silence.

"After our Bible teaching, we light our special candle, which is always placed in the center of our circle on a little bench covered with our strawberry tablecloth. We sit quietly around the lighted candle for a couple of minutes and allow the love of Jesus to bring peace to our hearts. The lighted candle represents the living, lov- ing presence of Jesus in our lives. During our times of prayer in silence, the presence of Jesus is very real to us.

"After our silence, we pray. Sometimes we pray for the person on our right or left. Sometimes we pray spontaneously. And some- times the leader asks specific people to pray for other specific peo- ple in the group. Whatever way we follow, our hearts are nour- ished by the prayers of one another.

152. Special Times

"Another way we celebrate Jesus' presence is to use our imagi- nations. Sometimes we set an empty chair in our circle just for Jesus. That is His chair. Other times we imagine Jesus with His arms around one of us. We imagine the smile on His face, the warmth of His embrace, the joy of His laughter at our meal table.

"We have fun celebrating different people we love outside of our group. We make huge banners on which each person draws or writes whatever he or she desires. These banners are often very colorful and creative. Sometimes we make cards for people which are equally simple, charming and very touching.

"We celebrate by going on a trip or having a party together once a month. Our trips are usually all day. We may go to the zoo, a museum, a street fair or to the botanical gardens. We have gone to many places over the last four years.

"When several persons from the Sonshine Group became members of the church there was a lot of eager anticipation. Each person wrote his or her own membership sharing, saying why he or she wanted to join the church. After each person answered the membership questions, the congregation gathered around the group, placed hands on each and prayed. A celebration meal followed with a festive table in the center for the new members. There were lots of balloons and party favors. The celebration ended with everyone having communion together.

Retreats

"Retreats are another time of celebration. We go to a 'Faith and Sharing Retreat' (inspired by Vanier). At these retreats handicapped people are made to feel important and at the center. Each person is treated equally regardless of who he or she is. These have been very healing times for many in the Sonshine Group, and a time of deep integration and celebration with the wider body of Christ.

"Reba Place Church has more and more grown to include handicapped persons in the life of the Body. Handicapped persons are much more at the heart of our whole church celebrations, usually just by being present and joining in on Sunday morning worship, communion and weddings.

Celebrating Death

"We have also learned to celebrate death together. Last November, Arthur, one of our members, died. As a group we were able to work through our grief and loss and arrive at a place of deep gladness for him. We all knew that Arthur was home with Jesus, and happy to be there. Fairly often someone will still say, 'I wonder what Arthur is doing in heaven now.' Praise God! The resurrection is our greatest celebration."

Postscript

Who Are the Folks at Reba Place Church?

The founders of Reba Place church-community in 1957 were several families of Mennonite background who wanted to reclaim the Anabaptist vision of the common life and spirit of the early Christian church. The founders felt called to exemplify radical love and economic sharing in the midst of society, much as the early Christians had: those believers, being "one in heart and mind" shared everything they had, cared for needy persons among them and testified to the resurrection of the Lord Jesus (Acts 4:32–35).

Reba Place Fellowship, as it was called then, sought to do the work of Christ *as* the body of Christ. The work of the church, they taught, was to introduce people to Jesus Christ as Savior and Lord and to invite them into a "tangible, visible Body," a supportive environment where their needs as growing Christians could be met. The Fellowship was committed to simplicity of lifestyle, to working for peace and justice in its immediate neighborhood and in the world, and to being a "priesthood of all believers," in which each individual ministered to the body with his or her unique gifts.

For a ten-year period, Reba Place members all lived in common households of some 15 to 20 individuals. Now, however, most members live in independent housing units within several blocks of each other in south Evanston, just north of the Chicago city line. Today about half of Reba Place's 170 adult members share finances in a common treasury, while the other half handle their finances as independent family units.

In recent years Reba Place has expanded to include more diversity of lifestyles and financial commitments than it included at earlier points in its history, but the common life together continues to be exceptionally strong. Folks at Reba Place share a united approach to

183

raising children, helping neighbors and worshiping God. "People say they belong to a church," remarked one member. "We say we belong to each other; we belong to the Lord."

Reba Place is a peace church, affiliated with both the Mennonite Church and the Church of the Brethren. Embodying a fascinating mix of conservative theology and radical social activism, Reba Place Church includes members from many backgrounds, including Jewish, Catholic, Episcopalian, Presbyterian and Methodist, to name a few. In fact, the Reba community could be seen as a microcosm of American religious history, including elements of congregationalism, communalism, Anabaptism, evangelicalism, pacifism, activism and more.

Reba Place Church is not a remote utopian community of visionary seers. Because of its 30-year communal history, during which time many members shared their finances, it might be thought that life at Reba is only for fanatic, counterculture types. Such a perception, however, is false. Folks at Reba Place are radical in some ways, particularly in their ability to incorporate diversity into a wholesome, loving fellowship. But they are ordinary folk—teachers, doctors, social workers, business entrepreneurs—who are intentional about being involved in each other's lives. Community must be deliberately built, they say, since it can no longer be presupposed, as it was in semi-static, rural neighborhoods.

Many urbanites, having moved from their rural, extended family and church relationships, are at a loss in the city, amidst an array of ever-changing, shallow relationships. The reality is that community in the city must be created out of disparate pieces. It must be intentional and dynamic in order to prevail against disintegration.

So-called "public" and "private" spirituality have clearly cross-fertilized each other at Reba Place. There is a natural flow back and forth which has invigorated both arenas. Yet the nuclear family remains a distinct sub-unit in the church, carrying the most immediate responsibility for socializing children and giving them their earliest awareness of the life of the Spirit.

On coming to Reba Place, I expected to find a homogeneous group. I imagined that a community with such intentionality would be shaped into a monotone of commonality with little tolerance for differences. Unity which preserves diversity, however, is one of the most striking features of Reba Place life. And I am convinced that it is the worship life of the community that is at the heart of its success as a meeting place for a motley and varying band over the years. It is Reba's ability to celebrate Christ's presence in their life together that, like the hub of a wheel, holds the radiating spokes solidly together while freeing them to rotate in many directions.

Reba Place is obviously not a perfect church. Over the years several persons have left the church, disappointed or disillusioned. Nor have Reba Place folks established a perfected, static model of community life. There is constant tinkering going on, adjustments here, experiments there, an unceasing dialogue about how to more nearly meet everyone's need for fellowship and worship. Yet, despite its shortcomings, Reba Place has accomplished a rare convergence of religious traditions. Nowhere else, in my experience, have I seen such freedom to bring together strengths from Catholicism, Judaism and Protestantism, and to shape them into a new, cohesive tradition that has its own integrity and beauty. In its own way, Reba Place is recreating the history of worship. While remaining firmly rooted in the Mennonite and Church of the Brethren traditions, it hasn't hesitated to enrich that "low church" style with elements which have long been disregarded or overlooked as worship resources.

"Catholics have so much to give us," remarks Hilda Carper, a "native Mennonite" at Reba Place, "because they make use of colors, smells and symbols. Everything they do is dramatized. We adults are so word-oriented," she continues, "but children aren't. Children can more actively join in when we dramatize our worship in one way or another."

The same is true of Jewish festivities, notes Joan Vogt, also a "native Mennonite." Jewish celebrations incorporate many "physical, sensory aspects," she says, "which are fun and have theological significance. They lend themselves to wholistic and intergenerational dramatization of the traditional stories."

Folks at Reba Place, especially those "schooled" in low-church traditions, have been most eager to enrich their worship life from the spiritual culture that preceded their traditionally austere, separatist style of approaching God. "An awareness of the church calendar and its religious holidays," Hilda says, "connects us with Christians all over the world and down through the centuries."

At Reba Place, freedom to draw on the vast spiritual traditions of Judaism and Christianity, and the freedom to create new traditions, have been deliberately cultivated and encouraged by those in leadership. Virgil Vogt, a current elder at Reba Place, observes that the freedom which has characterized Reba's worship life for many years has made it possible for many individuals to express their gifts in creating original music, dance, drama, banners and poetry. Persons have grown in confidence and skill as their gifts have been nurtured. The worship life of the church has been shaped by the active participation of *many* individuals, rather than being imposed on the group by either a prescribed traditional pattern or a clerical monopoly on such decisions. Worship is truly participatory at Reba Place. Everyone gets in on the act.

Yet another characteristic of Reba Place worship life, Virgil notes, is the integrity and sincerity of the participants. "People really *love* God and each other," he says, "and it is the reality of those relationships that makes celebrations powerful."

It would be wrong to give the impression that a mere overhaul of the traditional "fabric and furniture" of a church will result in a more vibrant worship life. A new ritual or a different order of worship won't do wonders for a church that is unresponsive to the new wine of the Spirit. The biblical writer of II Timothy has some strong words for those who preserve the "form of godliness" but deny its power.

Folks at Reba Place know that true worship is filled with power—power that convicts, awakens, energizes. Rituals of worship merely give shape to a reality that is already stirring within those who have opened themselves, humbly and expectantly, to the Spirit of light and love.

Readings and Sources

Baille, John. *A Diary of Private Prayer*. New York: Scribner's Sons, 1949.

Boyer, Ernest Jr. *A Way in the World*. San Francisco: Harper & Row, 1984.

The Book of Common Prayer. New York: The Seabury Press, 1979.

Carmody, Denise Lardner. *Feminism and Christianity: A Two-Way Street*. Nashville: Abingdon, 1982.

Day, Dorothy. *The Long Loneliness: An Autobiography*. San Francisco: Harper & Row, 1952.

Deiss, Lucien. *Springtime of the Liturgy*. Collegeville, Minn.: The Liturgical Press, 1967.

Fynn. *Mister God, This is Anna*. London: Collins, 1974.

Gilkey, Langdon. *Message and Existence*. Minneapolis: The Seabury Press, 1979.

Greeley, Andrew M. *Religion, A Secular Theory*. New York: The Free Press, 1982.

Gustafson, David L. "Shalom: The Dream of Reality." The Congregational Resources Board of the Conference of Mennonites in Canada.

Hartz, Joseph. *Authorized Daily Prayer Book*. New York: Bloch Publishing Co., 1948.

Hebblethwaite, Margaret. *Motherhood and God*. London: Geoffrey Chapman, 1984.

Hopkins, Mary, O.P. *Celebrating: Family Prayer Services*. New York: Paulist Press, 1974.

Hunt, Gladys. *Honey For a Child's Heart*. Grand Rapids, Mich.: Zondervan Publishing House, 1969.

Jackson, Dave and Neta. *Living Together in a World Falling Apart*. Carol Stream, Ill.: Creation House, 1974.

Jones, Alan. *Exploring Spiritual Direction*. New York: The Seabury Press, 1982.

An Inclusive Language Lectionary: Readings for Years A, B, and C. Published for the Cooperative Publication Association. Atlanta: John Knox Press, New York: The Pilgrim Press, Philadelphia: The Westminister Press, 1984 and 1985.

Lawrence, Brother. *The Practice of the Presence of God*. Tappan, N.J.: Revell, 1969.

L'Engle, Madeleine. *A Circle of Quiet*. New York: The Seabury Press, 1972.

L'Engle, Madeleine. *The Irrational Season*. New York: The Seabury Press, 1979.

L'Engle, Madeleine. *Walking on Water*. Wheaton, Ill.: Harold Shaw Publishers, 1980.

Maloney, George. *Alone With the Alone*. Notre Dame: Ave Maria Press, 1982.

The Mennonite Hymnal. Scottdale, Pa.: Herald Press and Newton, Kan.: Faith and Life Press, 1969.

Merton, Thomas. *The Seven Storey Mountain*. Garden City, N.Y.: Image Books, 1970.

Micks, Marianne. *The Future Present*. New York: The Seabury Press, 1970.

Moltmann, Jurgen and Moltmann-Wendel, Elisabeth. *Humanity in God*. New York: The Pilgrim Press, 1983.

Mossi, John ed. *Bread Blessed and Broken*. New York: Paulist Press, 1974.

Nouwen, Henri J.M. *A Cry for Mercy: Prayers From the Genesee*. Garden City, N.Y.: Doubleday, 1981.

Nouwen, Henri J.M. *Making All Things New*. San Francisco: Harper & Row, 1981.

Ruether, Rosemary and Keller, Rosemary. *Women and Religion in America, Volumes 1-3*. San Francisco: Harper & Row, 1983.

Smart, Ninian. *In Search of Christianity*. San Francisco: Harper & Row, 1979.

Smith, Antionette and Leon. *Growing Love in Christian Marriage*. Nashville: Abingdon, 1982.

Thompson, Bard. *Liturgies of the Western Church*. Philadelphia: Fortress Press, 1980.

Underhill, Evelyn. *An Anthology of the Love of God*. Wilton, Conn.: Morehouse-Barlow, 1976.

Vanier, Jean. *Community and Growth*. New York: Paulist Press, 1979.

Walker, Georgiana ed. *The Celebration Book*. Glendale, Calif.: Publ. Division of G/L Publications, Regal Books.

Wood, Ralph C. "An Instinct for Orthodoxy and an Appetite for Truth," *Books and Religion*, Vol. 13, No. 8-9, Nov.-Dec. 1985.